STEW!
GENEVIEVE TAYLOR

**100 SPLENDIDLY
SIMPLE RECIPES**

First published in Great Britain in 2011
by **Absolute Press**
Scarborough House
29 James Street West
Bath BA1 2BT
Phone 44 (0) 1225 316013
Fax 44 (0) 1225 445836
E-mail info@absolutepress.co.uk
Website www.absolutepress.co.uk

Publisher Jon Croft
Commissioning Editor Meg Avent
Art Director Matt Inwood
Design Matt Inwood
and Claire Siggery
Editor Jane Bamforth
Photography Mike Cooper
Food Styling Genevieve Taylor

ISBN: 9781906650476

Printed and bound in China on
behalf of Latitude Press

A note about the text

This book was set using ITC Century
and Serifa. The first Century typeface
was cut in 1894. In 1975, an updated
family of Century typefaces was
designed by Tony Stan for ITC.
The Serifa font was designed by
Adrian Frutiger in 1978.

Thanks

Writing *Stew!* has been a total pleasure
and I have enjoyed it immensely.
I would like to say a huge thank you
to everyone at Absolute Press for
honouring me with the job of creating
all these lovely dishes. Thank you to
Jon Croft and Meg Avent for trusting
me to deliver and to Matt Inwood for
his general positivity and kind words
of encouragement throughout.

Thanks are also due to Mike Cooper
for his beautiful photographs.
Between us we tried to create food
that looks as good as it tastes, and it
is always a pleasure to work with such
a creative yet refreshingly faff-free
photographer.

This book is for my family. A huge
thank you to Rob, my gorgeous
husband who manages to stay
delicious despite being ridiculously
well fed during the making of this
book! And to my beautiful children,
Izaac and Eve, whom I love more than
I can say. And finally a special thanks
to my amazing Mum who let me boss
my way into her kitchen from a very
young age. It all started with the
chocolate crispy cakes and the
passion for cooking has kept on
growing ever since.

Stews, casseroles, braises, hotpots... these are all terms for essentially the same thing – the age-old method of cooking meat and vegetables gently in some sort of liquid. *Gently* is the key word here. None of the recipes in this book are what you'd call fast food and none are cooked over a high temperature or in a hot oven.

Cooking at such languorous speed is what gives you the most amazing flavours and textures. What I love most about stewing is that you take just a handful of ingredients and time and patience seem to perform a magic trick in the pot when you are not looking. This is easy-peasy cooking at its most delicious. I admit, for some of the more exotic and fragrant stews the ingredient list is a little longer but the principles are the same. You simply assemble everything in the right order and let the low heat do the work whilst you get on with something else.

The other thing I love about stews is their truly universal appeal. When I told my friends and family I was writing this book their answer was invariably the same 'I absolutely love stews, do you need any help with tasting?!'

I hope this book provides you with classic versions of old favourites but also that it opens your eyes to a wealth of new possibilities from all around the world.

Happy stewing!

Genevieve Taylor
Bristol, November 2010

BUY

In an ideal world we would all shop at our local butchers, fishmongers and greengrocers on a daily basis to source local, seasonal produce. But, as the mum of two young children, I know from personal experience that the supermarket often wins hands down on convenience. Therefore it was important to me that the majority of the ingredients in this book can be sourced in a one-stop-shop. However, I do have a great butcher and fishmonger that I use regularly, particularly to help to source the slightly more unusual ingredients. Quite often I will stock up on these harder to find things at the butchers or fishmongers and store them in the freezer until I want to use them. That way I can make something delicious with just a quick trip to the supermarket for a few last minute extras.

Choosing meat

The meat best suited for stewing comes from the more economical cuts, making this way of cooking eminently practical and sensible in cash-strapped times. But that doesn't make for cheap and bland eating. Meat for stewing tends to come from the harder working parts of the animal, like the muscles of the legs and neck, and with the proper treatment these parts yield a far superior taste than the pricier cuts.

There is one piece of advice I hope you will take seriously to heart as it does make a big difference. And that is to always try to buy your meat as a whole piece and cut it up yourself. Meat that is pre-diced potentially comes from all parts of the animal, and for that matter from all different animals. Each individual piece will therefore have different cooking requirements which will be impossible to meet within one pot. If you use a whole piece and prepare it yourself you know you are using the same cut of meat from the same beast and the cubes or slices will cook evenly to give the best results. With that in mind, below is a quick summary of the cuts to look out for when stewing:

Beef: shin, chuck steak, stewing steak, braising steak, skirt and oxtail
Pork: shoulder steaks, leg steaks and belly pork
Lamb: neck fillet, boned shoulder, shin and shank
Venison: shoulder, leg and flank
Chicken and feathered game: either a whole bird jointed, or legs or thighs

Choosing fish

Fish stews are another thing – they tend to be more uneconomical than the meat or vegetable varieties, and some can end up being really pricy! I think of fish stews as being a special treat to serve occasionally rather than as a regular family meal. When buying fish, freshness is the key. The eyes and skin should be shiny and bright, and the aroma should be of salty sea rather than overpoweringly fishy.

Often with fish stews the best policy is to choose the fish that look best at the fishmongers on the day you visit rather than to go with a fixed idea of the type of fish you need. Although for some recipes – the smoked fish chowder, for example – you will be asked to buy a specific thing. With smoked fish I tend to go for the undyed variety as I find the dyed versions a little lurid – but the choice is entirely yours.

Fish, in general, freezes well so if there is a special offer on a certain variety it is often a good idea to buy in bulk and freeze in recipe-sized quantities.

For me, the cooking of a stew is done in two distinct, but equally important, halves. Firstly, you apply a high heat to sear, caramelise and colour and ultimately to add flavour to the dish. Then you add the liquid – the stock, the wine, the water and reduce the heat to a minimum. It is during this long period of slow cooking that the complex flavours develop and grow.

Meat
When preparing meat, don't be too vigilant about removing all traces of fat and sinew. These elements, whilst a little unsightly when raw, will add bags of flavour to the dish when they break down during the long, slow cooking. The fat also adds body and viscosity to the final sauce, making it taste rich, smooth and unctuous. There is nothing worse than a watery, thin, flavourless stew. And where there is little natural fat, as in some of the vegetarian or fish stews, you will often be asked to add it, usually in the form of generously drizzled extra virgin olive oil at the end. I really feel we shouldn't be afraid of oils and fats when natural and unprocessed, they often taste great. And, used in moderation, they are a powerful tool in the canny cook's box of tricks.

In most of these recipes the meat is seared first. This is a very important step and not to be rushed. The golden rules are to sear in batches, not to overcrowd the pan and also not to stir too often. Heat the oil until its smoking, throw in the meat a few pieces at a time and leave it alone to colour and sear before turning it over. You are looking to brown, even slightly burn, the outside of the meat and that just won't happen it you titivate the pan's contents too frequently!

Fish
Fish in stews is treated in exactly the opposite way as meat. It is most often added at the last minute, so it gently poaches in the intensely flavoured liquor around it. For these stews it is the base, often of onions or other vegetables, that takes the time to cook, whilst the fish just takes a matter of minutes at the end. This means that fish stews in general are a lot quicker to prepare than meat ones.

Vegetables
A special mention must be made here for the vegetables in your stews. There is not a single recipe in this book, even the most carnivorous, that doesn't have at least one vegetable, if not more, at its heart. The one that features most often is the truly humble onion. It lends a wealth of characteristics: sweetness, mild astringency and deep savoury notes and is invaluable to slow cooking. Shallots and leeks offer similar properties. Whilst you will often be called to allow your onions to colour, never caramelise leeks or garlic as they will turn bitter if allowed to colour. The exception to this rule, and of course there are always exceptions in cooking as in life, is in south-east Asian cooking where they do colour their garlic and with great effect. Generally, though, it benefits from being left pale and interesting.

Pulses and beans
I adore pulses and beans and use them at every available opportunity. What's not to like? They are really cheap, very healthy and, cooked in the right way, incredibly tasty. You'll notice that most of the beans and pulses I specify are raw, dried ones. This is because the long, slow cooking in stock means the taste and texture becomes quite exquisite. But by all means substitute ready-cooked tins if that is what you have to hand. You will need to reduce the cooking time and the quantities of liquid accordingly. But I would urge you to use dried ones if you can, the result will be worth it.

Make ahead

All meat stews genuinely benefit from being made the day before they are eaten, which makes them perfect for prepare-ahead dinners. The flavours mature and develop, making them even more delicious when reheated. There is also the added bonus of being able to skim excess fat off a cold stew before heating it up allowing you to create a healthier dish.

Freeze

Meat stews freeze well and because of the length of time it takes to cook a good meat stew it makes sense in my mind to do an extra batch for the freezer. That way you have the benefit of a little slow-cooked comfort on those week nights when you just can't face the slow cooking but are in desperate need of the comfort.

Stews with pulses and beans also freeze excellently and there is something truly wonderful about finding a bag of deliciously warming beans in the freezer for lunch on a cold winter's day. Fish stews really don't reheat or freeze well, so they are best saved for the days when you have time to both prepare and eat them.

And one really important factor when freezing stews, and I know it sounds dull, but I would urge you to label it properly! I speak from a wealth of personal experience. I have lost count of the number of times I have put a bag or box in the freezer convinced I will remember what it is only to unearth it a couple of months later with no clue to its contents. I recently defrosted a tub of almond frangipane leftover from a Bakewell tart for my children's tea thinking it was mashed potato – enough said!

I tend to freeze food in labelled bags as I find I can pack them neatly into my freezer, but labelled plastic containers are good too. You can freeze stews as individual portions, (if you have a little leftover, for example), or as a complete family-sized meal. In both cases I would not freeze them for longer than 3 months in a deep freeze as the flavour may start to deteriorate after time – and so a date on you bag or box is essential.

When thawing food it is best to leave it overnight in the fridge to thaw gently and throughly. If you don't have time to do that then a few hours defrosting at room temperature is perfectly acceptable providing you check it has thawed all the way through before you begin reheating. As an emergency I would also use a microwave to thaw food on the defrost setting, but again you need to ensure it has properly defrosted before you begin to reheat it.

And reheat...

The rules for gentle cooking that you carefully followed when making your stew must also be applied with the same vigilance when reheating. There is no point spending two or three hours cooking the dish only to reheat it for five minutes on high in the microwave. All the hard work of relaxing the meat fibres over a long period of time will be totally and utterly destroyed by the unforgiving blast of the microwaves. You will end up with tough and shrunken pieces of rubbery meat, not the soft and yielding meat you started out with. Not that there is anything intrinsically wrong with reheating in a microwave. Just do it with patience. Use 50–60% of the power rather than 100% and allow it to do its job more slowly. A family-sized dish of stew will take around 15 minutes to reheat on medium power, and stir every now and then to ensure it is reheating evenly. Better still that you reheat your stew in a pan over a very low heat, or in a warm (160°C) oven. It will take longer but you will be well rewarded for lack of haste. It is hard to be specific about reheating times as there are too many factors to take into consideration – for example, the temperature of the food when you start to reheat, whether it was fridge-cold or at room temperature, the depth of the pan or bowl you are reheating it in. All are factors that will change the amount of time the stew takes to reheat. So the best advice I can give is to keep stirring and checking the stew until you are sure it is piping hot throughout. The way I tell if food is really piping hot is to give it a good stir with a metal spoon then touch the tip of the spoon to your lip. If you can only hold it there for a mere second or two it is hot enough to eat safely.

TRADITIONAL AND HEARTY

Some dishes are just classics – the ones that have been around for ever and are passed down from generation to generation, with little tweaks and adjustments made here and there. And some stews are utterly nostalgic and the mere smell of them will remind you of home and happiness. These really traditional, hearty recipes are the ones we find ourselves turning to time and time again, and that is the reason you find them here, right at the front of this book.

Beef stew with herby dumplings

When you say stew, this is probably the dish most people they will think of – a proper old-fashioned meat stew with tasty dumplings. Nothing fancy, nothing mucked about with, just good, honest, delicious food to serve to your family. This is great served simply with some buttered green vegetables – savoy cabbage or spring greens would be perfect.

Serves 4–6 | Takes 15–20 minutes to make, 2$\frac{1}{2}$ hours to cook

900g beef shin, cut into 3cm cubes
2–3 tbsp vegetable oil
2 large onions, chopped
2 large carrots, cut into large chunks
1 heaped tbsp flour
500ml beef stock
1 bay leaf
1 tsp dried thyme
2 tbsp Worcestershire sauce
1 level tbsp Marmite
salt and freshly ground black pepper

For the dumplings
200g self-raising flour
100g vegetable suet
2 tsp dried mixed herbs

Heat 2 tablespoons of the oil in a large, flameproof casserole dish until it is smoking hot. Fry the beef, a few pieces at a time, to a really rich dark colour. As each piece of beef is done remove it with a slotted spoon, to a plate and continue until the beef is browned.

Add a little more oil if necessary and fry the onions and carrots until they begin to soften and colour a little at the edges. Return the meat to the pan and add the flour, stirring it thoroughly to soak up the juices.

Pour in the stock, add the bay leaf, thyme, Worcestershire sauce and Marmite and bring everything slowly up to simmering point. Season well and cover with a lid or tight-fitting piece of foil. Transfer to the oven and cook for 2 hours or so by which time the meat should be really soft.

Mix all the dumpling ingredients together in a bowl and season well. Add just enough cold water to form a stiff but elastic dough. Divide the dough into 8–10 even pieces and roll into balls. Set aside on a plate.

When the stew is ready, remove from the oven and gently float the dumplings on the surface. Return the casserole dish to the oven, uncovered, and cook for around 20–25 minutes by which time the dumplings should be crisp on the surface and soft and fluffy inside.

Serve immediately while still bubbling hot.

Freeze the stew, but not the dumplings, for up to 3 months. Defrost in the fridge overnight before reheating thoroughly in the oven at 180°C/gas 4. Make the dumplings as in the method above and add when the stew is bubbling hot, then proceed as per the recipe above.

Coq au vin

This lovely French classic has stood the test of time with no surprise – it's rich, delicious and truly simple to make. I like to serve this with crusty French bread.

Serves 4–6 | Takes 15 minutes to make, $1^1/_2$ hours to cook

1 tbsp olive oil
1 x 1.8–2kg chicken, jointed into
    6 pieces
200g smoked streaky bacon, diced
12 shallots, peeled and left whole
250g chestnut mushrooms,
    quartered
2 cloves garlic, crushed
2 bay leaves
2 sprigs of fresh thyme
1 x 750ml bottle red wine
Salt and freshly ground black
    pepper
1 tbsp plain flour
1 tbsp softened butter
handful of fresh flat-leaf parsley,
    roughly chopped, to garnish
crusty french bread, to serve

Heat the oil in a deep, heavy-based frying pan (with a lid) that will fit the chicken in a single layer. Fry the chicken pieces on both sides until they are nicely golden. You may need to do this in a couple of batches. Once the chicken has browned remove it to a plate and set aside. Add the diced bacon and shallots to the pan and fry until they begin to get a little colour, then add the garlic and fry for a further minute

Return the chicken to the pan, along with the mushrooms and herbs and season with a little salt and freshly ground black pepper. Pour over the wine and bring slowly up to a gentle simmer. Cover and cook very gently for about $1^1/_2$ hours or until the chicken is tender and beginning to fall off the bone.

Combine the flour and butter to form a smooth paste (a beurre manié).

Carefully remove the chicken to a plate and set aside whilst you thicken the sauce. Add the beurre manié to the pan and stir constantly until it melts. Turn up the heat to a rapid boil and cook for 5 minutes. Reduce the temperature and simmer steadily until the sauce is glossy and thick enough to coat the chicken.

Serve the chicken with the sauce poured over and a generous scattering of flat-leaf parsley. A great mound of buttery mashed potato would be the perfect accompaniment.

Freeze for up to 3 months. Defrost overnight in the fridge before reheating thoroughly.

Boeuf bourguignon

This '60s and '70s dinner party classic is making a well deserved comeback! Marinating the beef overnight helps to give it an extra intense flavour, but, if you are really short of time, skip this step, or just leave it to marinate for as long as possible. This is delicious served with mashed root vegetables – I like a combination of parsnip and swede mashed with plenty of butter. But celeriac or mashed carrot would be great too.

Serves 4–6 |Takes 20 minutes to make, plus marinating 2½ hours to cook

**1kg beef skirt, cut into 3–4cm
cubes
1 x 750ml bottle red wine
3 cloves garlic, crushed
3 sprigs of fresh thyme
2 tbsp olive oil
10 shallots, peeled and left whole
500g chestnut mushrooms,
quartered
200g smoked pancetta, cubed
1 heaped tbsp plain flour
salt and freshly ground black
pepper
mashed root vegetables, to serve**

In a large non-metallic bowl, mix the beef with the red wine, garlic, thyme and a seasoning of salt and freshly ground black pepper. Leave to marinate in the fridge for as long as possible, overnight if you have time.

When you are ready to begin cooking the bourguignon, preheat the oven to 160°C/gas 3.

Remove the beef from the marinade, using a slotted spoon, reserving the marinade. Pat the beef dry on kitchen paper. Heat the oil in a large, flameproof casserole until smoking hot. Fry the beef, a few pieces at a time, until each piece gets a wonderful golden crust on the outside, transfer each piece to a plate as it is browned.

Turn the heat down a little and fry the shallots with the mushrooms and pancetta until they are beginning to soften and colour slightly. Sprinkle the flour into the casserole and return the beef to the pan along with the reserved marinade. Give everything a really good stir and bring up to a gentle simmer.

Cover with a lid and cook in the oven for 2½ hours, after which time the beef should fall apart when teased lightly with a fork. If the sauce is looking a little thin towards the end of cooking time, remove the lid to allow it to thicken slowly. If you have removed the lid you will need to stir it a few times to ensure the beef gets evenly cooked.

Taste to check the seasoning and serve piping hot with plenty of mashed vegetables.

Freeze for up to 3 months. Defrost overnight in the fridge before reheating thoroughly.

Simple chicken casserole

This is so simple – a handful of ingredients and literally a few minutes to assemble is all you need. Then you leave it to work wonders in the oven whilst you get on with something else. This is one of those meals I turn to when I don't feel like cooking and all I really want to do is sit on the sofa with a large glass of wine and the newspaper!

Serves 4–6 | Takes 10 minutes to make, 1¹/₂–2 hours to cook

2 tbsp plain flour
900g chicken thighs, bone in
 and skin on
2 tbsp olive oil oil
2 onions, chopped
2 carrots, chopped
2 tsp dried mixed herbs
300–400ml chicken stock
salt and freshly ground black
 pepper
mashed potatoes and green
 vegetables or crusty bread, to
 serve

Preheat the oven to 160°C/gas 3.

Season the flour with salt and freshly ground black pepper. Coat the chicken thighs in the seasoned flour. Place the oil in a large, flameproof casserole and heat it to smoking hot . Fry the chicken pieces until they are brown and golden on both sides.

Add the vegetables and herbs and enough chicken stock to just cover everything. Bring up to a simmer, cover with a lid and cook in the oven for 1¹/₂–2 hours or until the chicken and vegetables are tender and soft.

Serve with mashed potatoes and green vegetables or just a generous hunk of buttered crusty bread if even that is a step too far!

Freeze for up to 3 months. Defrost overnight in the fridge before reheating thoroughly.

Goulash

This Hungarian classic is sweet with peppers and paprika and seasoned with a hint of the unusual spice, caraway. I love to serve this simply with plain rice.

Serves 4–6 | Takes 15 minutes to make, 2 hours to cook

2 tbsp olive oil
800g braising beef, sliced into 5cm strips
1 onion, sliced
2 cloves garlic, crushed
2 tbsp paprika
2 tsp caraway seeds, roughly ground
400g can chopped tomatoes
500ml water
2 red peppers, sliced into strips
150ml soured cream
salt and freshly ground black pepper
boiled rice, to serve

Heat the oil in a large heavy-based pan and brown the beef a few strips at a time. Remove the strips to a plate and continue until all the beef has been browned.

Return the browned beef to the pan and add the onion, paprika and ground caraway seeds. Fry for a few minutes until the onions are just beginning to soften.

Pour in the tomatoes and 500ml water and season with a little salt and pepper. Bring up to a steady simmer, reduce the heat to as low as possible, cover with a lid and cook very gently for $1\frac{1}{2}$ hours.

Add the peppers, stir thoroughly and cook for a further 30 minutes (if the sauce is a little thin at this stage, leave off the lid for the final 30 minutes of cooking to allow it to thicken) or until the beef is tender and the peppers are soft.

Remove from the heat and stir through the soured cream. Taste to check the seasoning and adjust if necessary. Serve with plenty of rice to soak up the delicious sauce.

Not suitable for freezing as the peppers loose their texture and become soggy.

Beef in Guinness

The Guinness in this traditional stew not only serves to tenderise the meat but it also adds a rich flavour that works brilliantly to warm you from the inside out on cold winter nights. Creamy mashed potato is all you really need to serve alongside to soak up the lovely juices.

Serves 4–6 | Takes 15 minutes to make, 2 hours to cook

900g braising beef or beef shin
2 tbsp plain flour
2 tbsp vegetable oil
1 large onion, sliced
2 carrots, cut into wedges
1 parsnip, cut into wedges
500ml Guinness
2 bay leaves
splash of Worcestershire sauce
salt and freshly ground black pepper
mashed potato, to serve

Cut the beef into approximately 3cm chunks, trimming off some of the fat if necessary do keep a little fat on though, it'll add to the body and flavour of the dish. On a large plate, season the flour with a little salt and pepper and toss the beef in the flour to thoroughly coat each piece.

Add the oil to a large, flameproof casserole and heat until it is smoking. Fry the beef a few pieces at a time, turning each piece to get a good brown colour. Do this in batches, removing each piece to a plate as it is done, so you don't overcrowd the pan. You want the meat to fry rather than sweat, the caramelised and even slightly burnt bits will add great flavour to the finished dish.

Return the meat to the casserole and add the onion, carrot and parsnip and fry for a couple more minutes Pour over the Guinness and add the bay leaves and Worcestershire sauce. Bring up to a gentle simmer, cover with a lid and cook as gently as possible for around 2 hours, by which time the meat will be soft and almost falling apart. Taste to check the seasoning and add a little salt and pepper if necessary.

Defrost overnight in the fridge before reheating thoroughly in the oven at 160°C/gas 3. Heating in the oven prevents the parsnip and carrots breaking up too much on reheating.

Lancashire lamb hotpot with braised red cabbage

This is traditional eating at its best – the rich hotpot is wonderfully complemented by the slightly sweet and sour cabbage. Just the sort of thing you want to eat on a bracing winter's day after an afternoon on the hills or standing on the touchline!

Serves 4–6 | Takes 25 minutes to make, 2³/₄ hours to cook

2 tbsp plain flour
1kg lamb neck fillet, cut into 3cm
   cubes
2–3 tbsp olive oil
700g onions, sliced
1 tsp dried mixed herbs
1 kg potatoes, peeled and sliced
   into 5mm rounds
500ml lamb or vegetable stock
50g butter, diced
salt and freshly ground black
   pepper

For the braised red cabbage
1 small red cabbage, finely sliced
2 red onions, finely sliced
1 cooking apple, peeled, cored and
   finely chopped
4 tbsp red wine vinegar
4 tbsp brown sugar
1 tsp mixed spice
50g butter, diced

Preheat the oven to 160°C/gas 3.

Season the flour with salt and freshly ground black pepper. On a large plate, toss the lamb in the seasoned flour to coat it evenly all over.

Heat 2 tablespoons of the oil in a large, flameproof casserole and fry the lamb all over to get a lovely golden crust. Do this in two or three batches, setting aside the browned pieces on a plate as they are ready.

Add a splash more oil to the pan if necessary and fry the onions with the

herbs for 4–5 minutes. You want them be soft, golden and lightly caramelised. Return the meat to the casserole and give everything a really good stir.

Layer the potatoes over the top of the meat and pour over the stock. Dot the butter over the top and add a final seasoning of salt and black pepper. Cover with a tight-fitting lid and transfer to the lowest shelf of the oven to cook for 2 hours.

Once the hotpot is in the oven make the braised red cabbage. Lay the cabbage, onion and apple in a roasting tin, sprinkle over the red wine vinegar, brown sugar and mixed spice. Dot with the cubes of butter and season generously with salt and freshly ground black pepper. Pour over 100ml water and cover tightly with foil. Cook in the oven above the hotpot and stir once or twice during the cooking.

After the hotpot has been cooking for 2 hours, remove the lid, increase the temperature to 200°C/gas 6 and cook for a further 30–45 minutes to allow the potatoes to develop a lovely golden crust. At this point, check the braised red cabbage. It may need a splash more water if it is looking a little dry.

Serve the hotpot straight from the oven with the cabbage on the side.

Freeze both the hotpot and the cabbage separately for up to 3 months. Defrost overnight in the fridge before reheating thoroughly in the oven at 160°C/gas 3.

Highland lamb stew

The pearl barley in this hearty stew adds a delicious and slightly chewy texture that's hard to beat. Sometimes if I'm feeling extravagant, and it's very cold outside, I add a generous splash of whisky to the pan just before the end of cooking... and why not? This dish needs no accompaniment as its really very hearty, but if you fancied, a little generously buttered bread would be delicious to dip in the juices.

Serves 4–6 | Takes 15 minutes to make, 2 hours to cook

2 tbsp plain flour
800g lamb neck fillet, cut into 3cm
  cubes
2–3 tbsp olive oil
2 leeks, washed thoroughly and
  sliced
2 sticks celery, sliced
2 carrots, cut into 3cm chunks
$1/2$ swede, cut into 3cm chunks
1 litre lamb or vegetable stock
100g pearl barley
2 bay leaves
2 sprigs of fresh thyme
2 sprigs of fresh rosemary
salt and freshly ground black
  pepper

Season the flour with salt and freshly ground black pepper. On a large plate, toss the lamb in the seasoned flour to coat it evenly all over.

Heat 2 tablespoons of the oil in a large heavy-based pan and fry the lamb until well browned on all sides. Do this in two or three batches, setting aside the browned pieces on a plate, as they are ready.

Add a splash more oil if necessary and fry the leeks, celery, carrots and swede over a gentle heat until they soften a little. Return the meat to the pan, pour in the stock and stir through the pearl barley and herbs.

Bring up to a gentle simmer, cover with a lid and cook for around 2 hours or until the lamb is tender and the pearl barley plump and cooked. Towards the end of cooking you may need to add a splash of water if it is getting a little dry.

Taste to check the seasoning and serve steaming hot.

Defrost overnight in the fridge before reheating thoroughly in the oven at 160°C/gas 3. Heating in the oven prevents the swede and carrots breaking up too much on reheating.

Chicken pot au feu

Translating literally from the French as 'pot on the fire', this simple stew hails from the days when families had a simmering pot on an open fire that was added to day to day and never emptied. You took a bit out, you put a bit in, and it kept on going. Traditionally bits and pieces of beef would have provided the meagre meat element to this peasant dish. But these days we can afford to be a bit more generous, and I like to use a whole chicken as I like the way it sits, pale, plump and succulent in the middle of the delicately stewed vegetables.

Serves 4–6 | Takes 15 minutes to make, 1$\frac{1}{2}$ hours to cook

3 tbsp olive oil
1 x 1.5kg whole chicken
250g bacon lardons
200g shallots, peeled and left whole
250g Chantenay carrots, left whole
3 sticks celery, halved
600ml chicken stock
1 tsp dried thyme
2 bay leaves
salt and freshly ground black pepper

Preheat the oven to 180°C/gas 4.

Heat the oil in a large, flameproof casserole and sear the whole chicken on all sides. It doesn't need to be dark brown, just a little golden here and there. The bird in the finished dish is supposed to look pale and interesting! Remove the chicken to a plate and set aside.

Add the lardons to the casserole and fry until crisp. Then add the shallots, carrots and celery and cook for a few more minutes so they start to colour a little at the edges. Push the vegetables to the sides of the casserole and place the chicken in the middle. Pour over the stock, add the herbs and season generously with salt and black pepper.

Bring up to a gentle simmer, cover with a lid and cook in the oven for around 1$\frac{1}{2}$ hours by which time the chicken will be cooked and the vegetables tender. The sauce will be thin, similar to a broth. If you prefer a thicker consistency then carefully remove the chicken and vegetables to a serving dish and boil the sauce to reduce until it is as you like it.

Serve the chicken carved into chunky slices, with the vegetables on the side and the sauce poured over the top. Serve with plenty of French bread to mop up the abundant juices.

Not suitable for freezing.

Beef and mushroom carbonnade

This recipe is based on the traditional *Carbonnade Flamande* or Flemish beef in beer. It is really rich and satisfying. Sometimes it is served with large cheese-topped croutons but I like to serve it a little more simply with plenty of crusty French bread.

Serves 4–6 | Takes 20 minutes to make, plus overnight marinating, 2–2$\frac{1}{2}$ hours to cook

900g braising beef (skirt or chuck), cut into 3cm cubes
400ml dark beer, preferably Belgian
1 tbsp fresh thyme leaves
2 bay leaves
2 tbsp plain flour
50g unsalted butter
1–2 tbsp olive oil
500g onions, thickly sliced
2 cloves garlic, crushed
250g large dark mushrooms, thickly sliced
1 tsp dark brown sugar
salt and freshly ground black pepper
crusty French bread, to serve

Place the beef, beer and herbs in a large, non-metallic bowl and set it aside to marinate in the fridge overnight or for at least 6 hours.

When you are ready to begin cooking the carbonnade, preheat the oven to 160°C/gas 3.

Remove the beef from the marinade with a slotted spoon, reserving the beer and herbs. Pat the beef dry with kitchen paper and lay on a plate.

Season the flour with salt and freshly ground black pepper. Sprinkle the flour over the beef and toss well to thoroughly coat each piece.

Heat the butter and 1 tablespoon of the oil in a large, flameproof casserole until the butter begins to foam. Quickly sear the pieces of beef until they are well-browned all over. Do this in several batches, removing each piece to a plate as it is done.

Once all the beef has been browned, turn down the heat and gently fry the onions for a few minutes until they start to soften and colour a little at the edges. You may need to add a little more oil to the pan. Add the crushed garlic and cook for a further minute or so, taking care not to let it burn or the stew will be bitter.

Stir in the mushrooms and sugar and carefully pour over the reserved marinade (it may foam rather vigorously). Give everything a thorough stir and bring up to a gentle simmer and cover with a tight-fitting lid. Cook in the oven for 2–2$\frac{1}{2}$ hours, or until the meat is really soft and tender. Half an hour before the end of cooking check the consistency of the sauce. Traditionally it is served on the thin side but if you like a thicker sauce you may want to remove the lid towards the end of cooking to allow it to reduce and thicken.

Taste to check the seasoning and serve whilst piping hot, with French bread.

Freeze for up to 3 months. Defrost overnight in the fridge before reheating thoroughly.

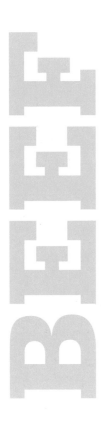

Steak and kidney casserole

This steak and kidney casserole is commonly used as the base of a warming hearty pie. I love to eat it like that, but I also like it as it is, served with mash and lightly steamed vegetables. When you just don't feel like making and rolling pastry and the filling is as delicious as this, frankly, why bother?

Serves 4–6 | Takes 15 minutes to make, 2–2$\frac{1}{2}$ hours to cook

2 tbsp plain flour
750g chuck steak, cut into 3cm cubes
400g ox kidney, trimmed and cut into 3cm cubes
2 tbsp vegetable oil
2 onions, chopped
250g chestnut mushrooms, thickly sliced
500ml beef stock
2 tbsp Worcestershire sauce
salt and freshly ground black pepper
mashed potato and steamed veg, to serve

Preheat the oven to 160°C/gas 3.

Season the flour and place it in a large bowl. Add the steak and kidney and toss it in the seasoned flour to get an even coating.

Heat the oil in a large flameproof casserole and brown the meats quickly on all sides. Do this in batches if necessary to avoid overcrowding the pan, set aside each batch on a plate while you continue until all the meat is done.

Return all the meat to the casserole, along with the onions and mushrooms. Fry for a few minutes until they start to soften then pour over the stock. Add the Worcestershire sauce and bring gently to a steady simmer. Cover with a lid and transfer to the oven. Cook for 2–2$\frac{1}{2}$ hours or until the meat is very tender.

Taste to check the seasoning, adding a little more salt and pepper if necessary, and serve piping hot with mash and your favourite steamed veg.

Freeze for up to 3 months. Defrost overnight in the fridge before reheating thoroughly.

Autumn pork stew

This is a stew I turn to on one of those first evenings at the very end of summer where you can smell autumn coming in on the breeze. Pork marries brilliantly with many fruits and this stew celebrates the early autumn glut of English pears. I would urge you to use perry (pear cider) if you can find it, it just feels like the right thing to do. But to be honest classic apple cider would be a perfectly delicious alternative.

Serves 4–6 | Takes 20 minutes to make, 1³/₄ hours to cook

2 tbsp plain flour
800g pork shoulder, cut into 3cm chunks
2 tbsp olive oil
2 onions, sliced
1 celery stick, finely diced
2 cloves garlic, crushed
500ml perry or cider
loose handful of fresh sage leaves, finely sliced
2 tsp English mustard
3 slightly unripe pears, peeled, cored, and quartered
salt and freshly ground black pepper
mashed potato, to serve

Season the flour with salt and pepper. Spread the pork out on a large plate and sprinkle over the seasoned flour. Toss the meat pieces around to coat them evenly in the flour.

Heat the oil in a flameproof casserole dish and fry the meat in batches until golden brown on all sides. Don't overcrowd the pan or the meat will sweat rather than fry. Set aside each batch on a plate while you continue until all the meat is done.

Once all the meat has browned return it to the pan and add the onions, celery and garlic and fry for a few minutes to allow the vegetables to soften a little.

Pour over the perry and stir through the sage and mustard. Bring the stew up to the boil and reduce the heat to a gentle simmer. Cover the pan and cook gently for around 1¹/₂ hours or until the pork is tender.

Add the pear quarters to the stew and continue to cook for around 15 more minutes or until they are soft but not disintegrating. You can leave the lid off at this stage if the sauce needs to reduce a little. Check the seasoning and add a little more salt and pepper if necessary. Serve with creamy mashed potatoes.

Defrost overnight in the fridge before reheating thoroughly in the oven at 160°C/gas 3. Reheating gently in the oven prevents the pears breaking up too much on reheating.

Ratatouille

Ratatouille is the traditional French Provençal stewed vegetable dish that became so popular, and so abused, in the '80s and at its worst it can be really very bland. I like to fry each vegetable separately and I don't cut them too small, so each retains its individual character. Unfortunately it takes longer to cook it this way but I think, when the vegetables are the showcase of the dish, the extra effort is worth it. Sometimes I eat this as a side dish to accompany roast chicken, or sometimes it's placed centre-table, with plenty of crusty bread to mop up the sauce.

Serves 4–6 | Takes 50 minutes to make, 1 hour to cook

5 tbsp extra virgin olive oil
2 red peppers, deseeded and cut into 4cm chunks
2 green peppers, deseeded and cut into 4cm chunks
2 courgettes, cut into 3cm slices
2 medium aubergines, cut into 3cm cubes
2 onions, sliced
3 cloves garlic, chopped
2 x 400g cans chopped tomatoes
1 tbsp herbes de Provence
salt and freshly ground black pepper
best-quality extra virgin olive oil, to serve

Preheat the oven to 180°C/gas 4.

In a large, flameproof casserole, heat 1 tablespoon of the olive oil and fry the red peppers over a high heat until they are lightly caramelised, this will take around 10 minutes. Stir them from time to time, but not too often or they won't take on enough colour. Transfer to a plate and set aside.

Repeat this step for the green peppers, courgettes, aubergines and onions. When it comes to the onions, add the garlic for a few seconds at the end of the frying time, but be careful not to burn it the casserole will be super-hot now.

Tip all the fried vegetables back into the casserole and pour over the tomatoes. Stir through the herbes de provence and season generously. Cover with a tight-fitting lid and transfer to the oven for around an hour, by which time the vegetables will be meltingly soft and the sauce thickened.

Taste to check the seasoning and adjust if necessary. Serve with a generous drizzle of your best extra virgin olive oil.

Not suitable for freezing.

Tuscan braised beef

In this rich Italian-style stew, pieces of braising steak are left in large pieces and studded with garlic before cooking, which adds an extra potency to the finished dish. This is great served with buttery polenta and some lightly cooked cabbage.

Serves 4–6 | Takes 20–25 minutes to make, 2$\frac{1}{2}$ hours to cook

1kg braising steak, cut into 5cm pieces
3 cloves garlic, peeled and cut into long strips
75g unsalted butter
1 tbsp olive oil
100g fatty pancetta, chopped
1 onion, finely chopped
2 carrots, finely diced
2 sticks celery, chopped
600ml beef stock
2 tbsp tomato purée
2 tsp dried oregano
sea salt and freshly ground black pepper
polenta and cabbage, to serve

Pierce the meat all over with the point of a sharp knife and insert the slices of garlic. Heat the butter and oil in a large, flameproof casserole and brown the beef in two or three batches, transferring each piece to a plate as it is done. Set the browned meat aside.

Add the pancetta, onion, carrot and celery to the casserole and allow to soften for a few minutes, stirring occasionally.

Pour over the stock, stir in the tomato purée and oregano and season with salt and pepper. Bring to a gentle simmer, cover and cook very gently for 2$\frac{1}{2}$ hours by which time the pieces of braising steak should be really tender and the sauce should be thickened. If the sauce is still a little thin by the time the meat is ready, remove it to a warm plate and boil the sauce rapidly until the desired consistency is reached.

Check the seasoning and adjust if necessary. Arrange the meat on a serving platter with the sauce poured over and serve with the polenta and cabbage.

Freeze for up to 3 months. Defrost overnight in the fridge before reheating thoroughly.

Hearty sausage hotpot

This is a really delicious family-friendly stew. It's very economical and adults and kids alike love it, especially when served with great mounds of spaghetti and lots of grated cheese.

Serves 4–6 | Takes 20 minutes to make, 1 hour to cook

1 tbsp olive oil
12 good-quality, thick pork
    sausages
2 carrots, finely diced
1 onion, sliced
1 celery stick, finely diced
1 clove garlic, crushed
2 x 400g cans chopped tomatoes
1 tbsp tomato purée
1 tsp dried oregano
salt and freshly ground black
    pepper
spaghetti and grated cheese,
    to serve

Place the oil in a heavy-based pan (with a tight-fitting lid) over a medium heat. Cut each sausage into three and fry gently in the oil until they take on a lovely golden colour. Resist the temptation to stir too much or they will never get crispy, they will take a good 10 minutes to cook.

Once the sausages are ready, add the carrots, onion, celery and garlic and gently sweat for a few minutes. Pour in the tomatoes and add the tomato purée and oregano. Season with a little salt and freshly ground black pepper and bring up to a steady simmer. Turn down the heat, cover with the lid and cook gently for around an hour or until the vegetables are tender and the sauce is thick and rich.

Serve over spaghetti and top with plenty of grated cheese.

Freeze for up to 3 months. Defrost overnight in the fridge before reheating thoroughly.

Oxtail with wine and herbs

I think of this as a winter weekend stew. It's so rich that in an ideal world you would only eat this when there was snow on the ground and frost in the air. But in reality, save it for any bitterly cold day when you have the time to let it slowly, slowly cook. The aromas that fill your home will be amazing and your patience will be well rewarded. Oxtail is an amazingly rich and delicious meat which seems to be making something of a well deserved comeback. Once a butcher's shop speciality, I have even seen it recently in my local supermarket. Serve very simply with mashed potatoes.

Serves 4–6 | Takes 20 minutes to make, 4–5 hours to cook

2 tbsp plain flour
1.5kg oxtail, jointed into pieces
2–3 tbsp olive oil
2 onions, sliced
2 carrots, sliced thickly
2 parsnips, sliced thickly
2 sticks celery, sliced
350g swede, cut in 4cm chunks
400ml red wine
3 tsp dried mixed herbs
salt and freshly ground black
   pepper
mashed potatoes, to serve

Preheat the oven to 150°C/gas 2.

Season the flour with salt and pepper. Lay the oxtail on a large plate and coat each piece in the seasoned flour.

Heat 2 tablespoons of the oil in a flameproof casserole and brown the oxtail on both sides until it is golden. You will need to do this in two or three batches so you don't overcrowd the pan. Remove to a plate and set aside.

Add a little more oil to the casserole, if necessary, and fry the onions, carrots, parsnips, celery and swede for a few minutes to soften slightly. Return the oxtail to the pan and pour in the wine and 400ml water. Add the herbs and give everything a good stir. Bring up to the boil, cover with a tight-fitting lid and transfer the casserole to the oven. Cook in the oven for anything between 4–5 hours or until the oxtail comes away from the bone easily when teased with a fork. Towards the end of cooking check there is enough liquid, if it is getting a little dry top up with a splash more water.

Check the seasoning and add a little more salt and pepper if necessary. Serve with plenty of mashed potatoes.

Defrost overnight in the fridge before reheating thoroughly in the oven at 160°C/gas 3. Reheating gently in the oven prevents the vegetables breaking up too much on reheating.

BEEF

Lamb with butternut squash and herbs

This is a really easy and tasty stew. I always leave butternut squash unpeeled as, to be honest, I am too lazy to peel it and it always seems so tricky to remove the thick skin safely and quickly. But I have to say I enjoy the slightly chewy texture it gives the finished dish. I like to eat this stew with a properly baked potato – by which I mean one baked in the oven rather than the microwave – dotted with plenty of butter.

Serves 4–6 | Takes 15–20 minutes to make, 2–2$\frac{1}{2}$ hours to cook

2 tbsp plain flour
800g lamb neck fillet, cut into 3cm cubes
2 tbsp olive oil
2 onions, sliced
2 cloves garlic, crushed
600ml lamb or beef stock
3–4 sprigs of fresh thyme
8–10 fresh sage leaves, roughly chopped
2 bay leaves
1 small butternut squash, cut into 3–4cm chunks
salt and freshly ground black pepper

Season the flour with salt and freshly ground black pepper. Spread the lamb out on a large plate, sprinkle over the flour and toss the pieces to coat evenly.

In a large, heavy-based pan, heat the oil until smoking hot. Sear the lamb in batches until golden brown and crispy, setting each piece aside on a plate as it is done.

When all the meat is browned, reduce the heat and fry the onions for a few minutes until they begin to soften, then add the garlic and cook for a further minute.

Return the lamb to the pan, pour over stock and add the thyme, sage and bay leaves. Bring up to a gentle simmer, cover with a lid and cook for 1$\frac{1}{2}$ hours.

Add the chunks of squash, re-cover and continue to cook until the meat and squash are tender. This will take between 30 minutes to 1 hour.

Taste to check the seasoning and adjust if necessary.

Freeze for up to 3 months. Defrost overnight in the fridge before reheating thoroughly in the oven at 160°C/gas 3. Reheating gently in the oven prevents the squash breaking up too much on reheating.

PORK

Bacon and split pea hotpot

This is hearty stew making at its best, just the sort of thing to come home to after a bracing winter walk. After you assemble it you simply put it in the oven and leave it to cook quietly by itself. It will be ready after a couple of hours but it will be happy to cook for up to 3 hours if necessary. This dish needs no accompaniment other than lots of generously buttered crusty bread.

Serves 4–6 | Takes 15 minutes to make, 2–3 hours to cook

2 tbsp vegetable oil
600–700g bacon joint, cut into 2cm chunks
1 onion, chopped
2 carrots, chopped into chunks
2 sticks celery, finely chopped
$1/2$ swede, peeled and chopped into chunks
250g split peas
1 litre vegetable stock
1 bay leaf
$1/2$ tsp ground mace
salt and freshly ground black pepper
crusty bread, to serve

Preheat the oven to 160°C/gas 3.

In a large, flameproof casserole heat the oil and add the chopped bacon. Fry for a few minutes until the bacon is just starting to take on a little colour. Add the onion, carrot, celery and swede, followed by the split peas and vegetable stock and bring up to a steady simmer. Lastly, throw in the bay leaf, the mace and season well with freshly ground black pepper. Do not add any salt at this stage as the bacon may be salty enough.

Cover with a tight-fitting lid and transfer to the oven to cook for around 2 hours after which the bacon will be coming apart if teased gently with a fork and the split peas will be soft. Remove the lid for the final 30 minutes of cooking if the hotpot is look a little liquid. You are looking for a thick, soupy texture. Check the seasoning and add more pepper and salt, if desired.

Serve with lots of crusty bread.

Freeze for up to 3 months. Defrost overnight in the fridge before reheating thoroughly in the oven at 160°C/gas 3. Reheating gently in the oven prevents the vegetables breaking up too much on reheating.

Sweet and sour pork with peppers

This may not seem like a 'traditional' recipe in the truly British sense but I have included it here out of vaguely nostalgic feelings. I can't remember a specific occasion when I was served sweet and sour as a child but I do have memories of savoury dishes like this where tins of pineapple or mandarin oranges or dried raisins formed part of the ingredients.

Serves 4–6 | Takes 20 minutes to make, 1¹/₂ hours to cook

2 tbsp vegetable oil
800g pork shoulder, cut into 3cm cubes
1 tbsp cornflour
227g can unsweetened pineapple chunks, drained and juice reserved
2 tbsp tomato ketchup
2 tbsp malt vinegar
1 tbsp brown sugar
1 tsp ground ginger
2 onions, sliced
1 red pepper, deseeded and sliced
1 green pepper, deseeded and sliced
2 cloves garlic, crushed
200g can sweetcorn, drained
salt and freshly ground black pepper
boiled rice, to serve

In a large heavy-based pan, heat the oil and brown the pork over a high heat. Do this in batches and transfer the browned pieces of pork to a plate and set aside.

Whilst the meat is browning, mix the cornflour to a paste in a measuring jug with a little of the pineapple juice. Pour the rest of the juice into the jug, along with the ketchup, vinegar, brown sugar and ginger. Mix thoroughly and top up with cold water to get a total of 500ml of liquid. Set aside.

One the meat has browned, add the onion and peppers to the pan and fry over a medium heat for a few minutes until they begin to soften and colour a little at the edges. Add the crushed garlic and fry for another minute, then return the pork to the pan.

Pour over the juice mixture, stir really well and bring up to a steady simmer. Cover with a lid and simmer very gently for around an hour. Remove the lid and add the pineapple chunks and sweetcorn and simmer for a further 20–30 minutes or until the pork is tender. At this stage you can leave the lid off if the sauce is a little thin or re-cover it with the lid if it is not.

When the meat is cooked, taste the sauce and season with a little salt and black pepper. You may also need to add a little more vinegar and/or brown sugar to get the right balance of sweet and sour.

Serve with plenty of plain rice.

Not suitable for freezing as the peppers will become very soggy on defrosting.

Beef stroganoff

Traditionally beef stroganoff is made with fillet steak cooked very quickly. This version uses cheaper braising cuts cooked much more slowly. The resulting dish is more flavoursome, just as tender and a lot more economical. I like to eat this with wild rice and wilted greens.

Serves 4–6 | Takes 15–20 minutes to make, approximately 2$\frac{1}{2}$ hours to cook

2 tbsp olive oil
900g lean braising steak, cut into 3–4cm strips
2 large onions, sliced
2 cloves garlic, crushed
1 tbsp paprika
1 tsp cayenne pepper
$\frac{1}{2}$ tsp grated nutmeg
350g chestnut mushrooms
500ml white wine
200ml crème fraîche
salt and freshly ground black pepper
wild rice and wilted greens, to serve

Heat the oil in a large, heavy-based pan and quickly sear the beef on all sides until it is dotted here and there with a deep golden brown crust. Do this in batches to avoid overcrowding the pan, transferring each piece of meat to a plate as it is browned.

Add the onions to the pan and fry until lightly golden brown, then add the garlic, paprika, cayenne and nutmeg and fry for a further minute or so. Return the beef to the pan, along with any juices that may have accumulated on the plate. Stir in the mushrooms and wine. Season well and bring up to a steady simmer. Lower the heat to the minimum temperature. Cover with a lid and cook for 2–2$\frac{1}{2}$ hours or until the beef is really tender.

Using a slotted spoon, remove the meat to a plate and set aside. Raise the heat and reduce the sauce until thick and syrupy, then add the crème fraîche and return the meat to the pan. Lower the temperature and gently heat the meat until piping hot.

Taste to check the seasoning and serve with rice and wilted greens.

Freeze for up to 3 months. Defrost overnight in the fridge before reheating thoroughly.

MEAL IN A BOWL

Most stews are best eaten alongside some sort of starchy partner; a pile of fluffy mash or buttery polenta or a hunk of crusty bread are all perfect accompaniments. But these recipes come with the added bonus of some sort of bean, lentil or starchy vegetable included within the stew. Of course, crusty bread is still a delicious, albeit optional, extra! This is one pot cooking at its simplest, most comforting, best.

Fabada

This one-pot chorizo, morcilla and bean stew hails from Asturias in northern Spain, where it is very popular. It is incredibly easy to make, but the ingredients can be hard to find. The Asturians would use faba beans, which are like big, fat cannellini beans. They are nigh on impossible to find in the UK so I tend to substitute them pretty successfully with butter beans. Morcilla, or Spanish black pudding, is the other tricky ingredient to buy but it can be found in a good delis. If you can't find it I suggest you use a little extra chorizo instead.

Serves 4–6 | Takes 10–15 minutes to make, plus soaking, $1^{1}/_{2}$–$2^{1}/_{2}$ hours to cook

500g dried butter beans, soaked overnight in plenty of cold water, drained and rinsed
1 tbsp olive oil
250g smoked bacon lardons
3 large onions, sliced
3 cloves garlic, crushed
400g raw chorizo, halved if large or kept whole if small sausages
100g morcilla
1 tsp smoked paprika
2 bay leaves
salt and freshly ground black pepper
generous handful of fresh flat-leaf parsley, roughly chopped (optional), to garnish

In a large, heavy-based pan, heat the olive oil and fry the lardons until they are just beginning to crisp a little. Add the onions and continue to fry until they are soft and just beginning to colour at the edges. Then add the garlic, chorizo, morcilla and the drained beans. Completely cover the beans with cold water and bring to a steady simmer.

Stir through the paprika, tuck in the bay leaves and season with plenty of black pepper but no salt at this stage, as it will make the bean skins tough. Cook at a steady simmer for $1^{1}/_{2}$–$2^{1}/_{2}$ hours, skimming off any scum if it appears on the surface. Throw in a few spoonfuls of cold water from time to time to ensure the beans stay submerged and cook properly. The stew is ready when the beans are exceptionally tender but not collapsing – this will vary widely according to the beans you use so it's best to keep an eye on it.

Taste and add salt and a little more black pepper as required. I like to serve this with a scattering of chopped flat-leaf parsley which isn't traditional but adds a certain freshness to what is rather a rich dish.

Freeze the stew for up to 3 months. Defrost overnight in the fridge before reheating thoroughly, adding a splash more water if it looks dry.

Lebanese-style bean stew with minted yogurt

This vegetarian dish uses a classic middle Eastern ingredient, pomegranate molasses and I urge you to find it for it adds a delicious sweet-sour note to the finished dish. These days it's fairly widely available, try looking in the spice aisle or speciality ingredients section of your supermarket.

Serves 4–6 | Takes 15 minutes to make, plus soaking, 1–1$\frac{1}{4}$ hours to cook

450g dried cannellini beans, soaked overnight in plenty of cold water, drained and rinsed
2 tbsp olive oil
1 large onion, sliced
4 large cloves garlic, sliced
2 tsp ground cumin
1 tsp cinnamon
3 cloves
1.5 litres vegetable stock
2 tsp pomegranate molasses
300g green beans, topped and tailed

For the minted yogurt
250ml Greek yogurt
handful of fresh mint leaves, chopped, plus a little extra to garnish
salt and freshly ground black pepper

Heat the oil in a large, heavy-based pan and fry the onion over a medium heat until it starts to soften. Turn up the heat and allow the onion to caramelise a little before adding the garlic and spices. Fry for a couple of minutes until the spicy aromas waft into the air, then add the beans. Add the stock and pomegranate molasses, bring to the boil and allow to boil rapidly for a good 10 minutes. This step is important as it ensures the beans are properly cooked.

Reduce the heat to a steady simmer and cover with a lid. Cook for around 1 hour or until the beans are soft. Stir through the green beans, re-cover and cook for 8–10 minutes by which time they should be soft and tender but with a little bite to them. Taste and season with salt and freshly ground black pepper.

Whilst the green beans are cooking, make the minted yogurt by simply stirring all the ingredients together.

Serve the bean stew in bowls topped with a generous dollop of minted yogurt and finish with a little extra chopped mint and a generous grinding of black pepper.

Freeze the stew (not the yogurt) for up to 3 months. Defrost overnight in the fridge before reheating thoroughly, adding a splash more water if it looks dry.

Italian sausage, fennel and lentil casserole

For this recipe, I like to use Lucanica sausage that I buy from my local traditional Italian deli. It comes in a roll, coiled up like a sleeping snake, and is spiced with black pepper and fennel seeds. If you can't find this specific type any Italian-style sausage would work very well. This recipe needs no accompaniment but you could follow it with a simple rocket salad.

Serves 4–6 | Takes 10 minutes to make, 40 minutes to cook

1 tbsp olive oil
400g spiced Italian sausage, sliced into 3–4cm lengths
1 tsp fennel seeds
1 fennel bulb, finely sliced
1 onion, finely sliced
2 cloves garlic, crushed
200g small brown or green lentils
175ml white wine
500ml chicken or vegetable stock
1–2 bay leaves
salt and freshly ground black pepper
generous handful of fresh flat-leaf parsley, chopped, to garnish

Heat the oil in a flameproof casserole and fry the sliced sausage until golden brown all over.

Lightly crush the fennel seeds using a pestle and mortar. Add them, along with the sliced fennel, onion and garlic to the casserole and continue to fry gently for about 5 minutes, until the vegetables start to soften.

Throw in the lentils and pour in the wine and stock, followed by the bay leaves. Bring everything up to the boil and then reduce the heat to a steady simmer. Cook, with the lid on, for about 40 minutes or until the lentils are tender but not falling apart. Stir occasionally during cooking to make sure the lentils aren't sticking. Remove the lid halfway though the cooking to thicken the sauce if necessary.

Season to taste, with salt and freshly ground black pepper, and serve in bowls with a generous scattering of parsley.

Freeze for up to 3 months. Defrost overnight in the fridge before reheating thoroughly in the oven at 160°C/gas 3. Reheating gently in the oven prevents the fennel breaking up too much on reheating.

Provençal chicken, haricot bean and shallot casserole

Flavoured with herbs and lemon this dish is the very essence of the Mediterranean in a bowl. I love to eat this on slightly chilly summer evenings when you need a little warming up but don't want to lose the tastes of summer.

Serves 4–6 | Takes 15–20 minutes to make, 1½–2 hours to cook

2 tbsp plain flour
8–10 chicken thighs, bone in and skin on
2–3 tbsp olive oil
12 shallots, peeled and left whole
2 garlic cloves, crushed
250ml white wine
300ml chicken stock
410g can haricot beans, drained and rinsed
400g can chopped tomatoes
2 tsp herbes de Provence
2 wide strips of lemon peel
salt and freshly ground black pepper
generous handful of fresh flat-leaf parsley, roughly chopped and 2 tbsp small black olives, to garnish

Preheat the oven to 180°C/Gas 4.

Put the flour on a large plate and season well with salt and pepper. Roll the chicken thighs in the flour to coat all over.

In a large, flameproof casserole, heat 2 tablespoons of the olive oil and fry the chicken pieces, a few at a time, until they are golden on all sides. Remove the chicken to a plate as it is done and continue until they are all browned.

In the same pan, adding a little more oil if necessary, fry the whole peeled shallots until they are browning slightly. Add the crushed garlic and fry for 1 minute, taking care not to let it burn or it will make the dish bitter. Deglaze the pan by adding the white wine and stirring and scraping the bottom to release all the sticky caramelised bits.

Return the chicken to the pan, along with the stock. Add the haricot beans, tomatoes, herbs and lemon peel and bring everything to the boil.

Cover and cook in the oven for 1½–2 hours, until the chicken is really tender and falling off the bone. Serve in deep, wide bowls with a scattering of parsley and black olives.

Freeze for up to 3 months. Defrost overnight in the fridge before reheating thoroughly. You may need to add a little more water or stock during reheating if it looks a touch dry.

Cajun prawn and chorizo gumbo

There are literally thousands of ways to make a gumbo, the delicious spicy stew from the state of Louisiana. The essential base of the gumbo is the roux, a mix of flour and oil that is cooked until coffee-brown which acts not only as a thickener but also as a flavour enhancer.

Serves 4–6 | Takes 50 minutes to make, 1$\frac{1}{4}$–1$\frac{1}{2}$ hours to cook

2 tbsp vegetable oil
2 tbsp plain flour
3 sticks celery, finely chopped
2 large onions, chopped
2 green peppers, chopped
3 cloves garlic, crushed
4 large tomatoes, chopped
250g chorizo, cut into 1cm slices
750ml prawn stock (see below)
400g raw tiger prawns, heads and shells removed and reserved
400g fresh crabmeat, half brown and half white
75g white rice
3 tsp paprika
1 tsp dried thyme
1 tsp dried oregano
1 tsp cayenne pepper
1 tsp black peppercorns, crushed
salt and freshly ground black pepper

For the prawn stock
1 litre good-quality fish stock
prawn heads and shells (see above)
2 carrots, chopped
2 bay leaves
6 black peppercorns

Begin by making the prawn stock, put the fish stock into a pan along with the prawn heads and shells. Add the carrots, bay leaves and peppercorns and bring up to a steady simmer and cook, uncovered, for 30–40 minutes. Strain and set the stock aside.

Whilst the stock is simmering, start the gumbo by making the roux. Put the oil and flour into a heavy-based pan and cook gently for 15–20 minutes or until the roux is a deep, coffee brown colour.

At this stage, cook the rice in a small pan of boiling water for around 10–12 minutes or until tender. Drain and set aside.

Add the celery, onions and green peppers to the roux and cook for a few minutes until the vegetables start to soften. Then add the garlic, tomatoes, chorizo sausage and strained prawn stock. Bring to the boil and simmer, uncovered, for about an hour, after which the vegetables should be tender and the sauce thickened.

Add the prawns, crabmeat and cooked rice. Stir through the paprika, thyme, oregano, cayenne and peppercorns. Cook for a further 10 minutes or so until the prawns are cooked through.

Taste and season with salt and pepper, if necessary, and serve immediately.

Not suitable for freezing.

Lamb and butter bean stew with garlic-lemon breadcrumbs

Whilst this dish truly qualifies for meal-in-a-bowl status it is also special enough for informal entertaining. The succulent lamb and soft butter beans are contrasted beautifully by the crispy punchy garlic breadcrumbs. I really like the way that the different textures wake up your senses whilst you are eating.

Serves 4–6 | Takes 15 minutes to make, 2 hours to cook

**2 lemons
2 tbsp olive oil
700g lamb neck fillet, cut into
  2.5cm cubes
1 large onion, chopped
3 large cloves garlic, crushed
150ml white wine
2 x 400g cans butter beans,
  drained and rinsed
400ml lamb stock or water
2–3 sprigs of fresh rosemary
generous handful of fresh flat-leaf
  parsley, roughly chopped
salt and freshly ground black
  pepper**

**For the garlic-lemon crumbs
2–3 tbsp good-quality extra virgin
  olive oil
120g fresh white breadcrumbs
2 cloves garlic, finely chopped
flaked sea salt, such as Maldon,
  to taste**

Peel one long strip of peel from one of the lemons. Grate the remaining zest from the peeled lemon and the second lemon. Set the peel and zest aside.

Heat the oil in a flameproof casserole and quickly fry the cubes of lamb until they are golden brown all over. Add the onion and continue to fry for a few minutes until it begins to soften and colour a little at the edges. This slight caramelisation will add a lovely rich sweetness to the stew.

Throw in the garlic and cook for no more than a minute or so or it will burn and become bitter. Pour in the wine and allow it to evaporate for a few minutes before adding the butter beans, stock or water, rosemary and strip of lemon peel. Season with a little salt and pepper and bring everything up to a steady simmer. Cover, reduce the heat to as low as possible and cook gently for about 2 hours or until the lamb is falling apart and the butter beans are softly melting.

When the meat is ready, turn the heat off, stir through the parsley and allow the stew to sit for a few minutes to infuse whilst you make the garlic-lemon breadcrumbs.

For the breadcrumbs, heat the oil in a heavy-based pan and throw in the crumbs. Stir fry the crumbs so they get an even coating of oil and don't burn. Add a little more oil if they seem a little dry. This is the moment to use your best-quality oil, you really want the olive oil flavour to stand out proud. Once the crumbs are really crispy remove the pan from the heat and stir through the reserved lemon zest, garlic and crunchy salt.

Serve the stew in deep wide bowls sprinkled generously with the breadcrumbs and a really good grind of black pepper.

Freeze the stew for up to 3 months. Defrost overnight in the fridge before reheating thoroughly, adding an extra little water or stock if it is a bit dry. The garlic-lemon breadcrumbs best made fresh when you are ready to serve the stew – they would lose their pungency in the freezer.

Chicken with haricot beans and orange

To me this is a perfect late winter or early spring stew, full of soft melting wintery leeks but flavoured with a hint of orange, it seems to celebrate and embrace the shift in season. Sometimes I like to eat this on its own but it's also great with thick slices of garlic toast to soak up the zesty sauce.

Serves 4–6 | Takes 25 minutes to make, 1$\frac{1}{2}$ hours to cook

200g haricot beans, soaked overnight in plenty of cold water, drained and rinsed
2–3 tbsp olive oil
800g boneless chicken thighs, skin on
3 leeks, washed thoroughly and sliced
3 cloves garlic, sliced
1 litre chicken stock
200ml white wine
2 tbsp dried mixed herbs
1 orange, quartered
salt and freshly ground black pepper
bunch of fresh flat-leaf parsley, roughly chopped, to garnish

For the garlic toast
4–6 slices thick cut bread
50g butter, softened
2 cloves garlic, crushed
1 tbsp finely chopped parsley
salt and freshly ground black pepper

In a large, heavy-based pan heat 2 tablespoons of the oil and fry the chicken on both sides until golden brown and crisp skinned. You may need to do this in a couple of batches to avoid overcrowding the pan. Remove the chicken to a plate and set aside.

Turn the heat down to low, add a little more oil if necessary, and fry the leeks and garlic gently for a few minutes until they start to soften. Be careful not to burn the leeks charred leek are bitter and will ruin your stew.

Pour in the chicken stock and wine and bring to the boil. Add the beans and herbs and boil rapidly, uncovered, for 10 minutes. This is important to ensure the beans are cooked properly. After 10 minutes, turn the heat down to a steady simmer and add the fried chicken pieces along with the orange quarters. Season with plenty of freshly ground black pepper but no salt yet as it will toughen the bean skins. Cover with a lid and cook for an 1$\frac{1}{2}$ hours after which time the beans will be soft and the chicken meltingly tender. Check the level of stock towards the end of cooking, adding a few splashes of water if necessary to keep the beans submerged.

Remove the orange segments and taste to check the seasoning, it will definitely need some salt and maybe a little more black pepper. Serve immediately with a generous scattering of parsley.

Cooks tip
Make the garlic toast by grilling the bread on one side only. Mix the butter with the garlic and parsley, and season with a little salt and black pepper. Spread the garlic butter on the untoasted side of the bread and return to the grill. Cook until the bread is crisp and the butter melted and bubbling.

Freeze for up to 3 months. Defrost overnight in the fridge before reheating thoroughly. Add a splash of water or stock during reheating if it is a little dry.

Butternut squash and butter bean casserole with Parmesan dumplings

This hearty vegetarian casserole won't leave the meat lovers at your table yearning for a steak on the side. The initial roasting of the vegetables gives a really good depth of flavour which is wonderfully complemented by the super-savoury dumplings. Be prepared for cries of 'more please!'.

Serves 4–6 | Takes 40 minutes to make, 40 minutes to cook

1 medium butternut squash (approximately 600–800g), cut into 2.5 cm chunks (leave the skin on for added texture)
12 shallots, peeled and left whole
3 tbsp extra virgin olive oil
loose handful of fresh sage leaves, roughly chopped
1 heaped tbsp plain flour
3 cloves garlic, crushed
175ml white wine
400g can butter beans, drained and rinsed
2 tbsp sun-dried tomato purée
400ml vegetable stock
salt and freshly ground black pepper

For the Parmesan dumplings
200g self-raising flour
100g vegetable suet
3 heaped tbsp grated Parmesan cheese
2 tsp dried oregano

Preheat the oven to 220°C/gas 7.

Place the butternut squash and shallots in a roasting tin along with the olive oil, sage leaves and a little salt and pepper. Toss well to coat in the oil. Roast in the oven for 20–30 minutes until the vegetables are tinged with colour at the edges.

Whilst the squash and shallots are roasting make the dumplings by combining all the ingredients in a large bowl, season well. Add enough cold water, 1 tablespoon at a time, to bring it together to make a soft pliable dough, you will need 5–8 tablespoons in total. Shape the dough into 8–10 small balls and set aside.

When the squash and shallots are cooked, remove from the oven and turn the temperature down to 180°C/gas 4.

Add the flour to the roasting tin, stirring to coat the vegetables and soak up all the roasting juices. Add the garlic and white wine to the roasting tin, scraping at the bottom to release all the delicious sticky caramelised bits. Transfer the mixture to a casserole dish and add the beans, sun-dried tomato purée and vegetable stock and give everything a good stir.

Cover the casserole with a lid or tightly-fitting piece of foil and cook in the oven for 30 minutes. Remove from the oven and carefully add the dumplings so they float on the surface. Return to the oven, uncovered, for 20 minutes until the dumplings are crispy on the outside and fluffy and cooked through on the inside. Serve immediately while bubbling hot.

Not suitable for freezing.

Cavolo nero and cannellini beans with Gorgonzola toasts

This Italian-style bean and cabbage stew uses chicken stock and bacon to give it a rich deeply savoury taste. The Gorgonzola toasts add an intense flavour burst on the side. Do feel free to dunk them! Vegetarians can leave out the bacon and use vegetable stock instead.

Serves 4–6 | Takes 15 minutes to make, 1–1$\frac{1}{4}$ hours to cook

300g dried cannellini beans, soaked overnight in plenty of cold water, drained and rinsed
25g butter
1 tbsp olive oil
8 shallots, sliced
4 rashers smoked streaky bacon, chopped
2 cloves garlic, crushed
1.5 litre hot chicken or vegetable stock
250g cavolo nero, washed and sliced
Salt and freshly ground black pepper

For the Gorgonzola toasts
4 slices thick cut granary bread
125g creamy Gorgonzola cheese

Melt the butter gently with the olive oil in a heavy-based pan. Add the shallots and gently sweat for around 10 minutes or until they are really soft, then turn up the heat and allow then to caramelise. Once the shallots are a beautiful golden brown turn the heat back down, add the bacon and garlic and cook for couple of minutes, being careful not to burn the garlic or it will turn the stew bitter.

Add the hot stock and the drained cannellini beans and bring up to the boil and cover with a lid or tight-fitting piece of foil. Boil rapidly for 10 minutes this is important to make sure the beans are properly cooked. Reduce the heat, and simmer for 45 minutes – 1 hour or until the beans are cooked through.

Add the cavalo nero, stir through and cook for a further 10–15 minutes, uncovered, until it's tender to the bite.

Whilst the cavolo nero is cooking in the stew make the Gorgonzola toasts. Preheat the grill to high. Toast the bread on one side under the grill. Spread the Gorgonzola on the untoasted side and return to the grill for a minute or so until the cheese is melted and bubbling.

Season to taste with salt and freshly ground black pepper. Serve the stew in deep bowls with the toasts on the side.

If making ahead to freeze, prepare up until the point the cavalo nero is added, then cool and freeze for up to 3 months. Defrost in the fridge overnight and reheat thoroughly. Once hot add the cavalo nero and proceed as per recipe above. You may need to add a little water if it is a touch dry. Gorgonzola toast not suitable for freezing.

Brazilian black bean stew

This dish is based on Feijoada, the national dish of Brazil. The beans make up the bulk of this hearty stew, with smoked meat adding plenty of delicious flavour. You could eat this with a little chewy brown rice if you liked, although it's perfectly filling on its own.

Serves 4–6 | Takes 25 minutes to make, plus soaking, approximately 1$\frac{1}{2}$ hours to cook

500g dried black beans, soaked overnight in plenty of cold water, drained and rinsed
2 tbsp vegetable oil
2 onions, finely chopped
2 red or yellow peppers, deseeded and chopped
2 cloves garlic, crushed
225g smoked streaky bacon, chopped
225g chorizo, cut into 1cm slices
2 bay leaves
1 tsp smoked paprika
salt and freshly ground black pepper

To serve
small bunch of fresh coriander, roughly chopped
small bunch of fresh flat-leaf parsley, roughly chopped
4–6 tbsp soured cream
1 small orange, cut into wedges

Heat the oil in a large, heavy-based pan and fry the onions and peppers over a medium high heat until they begin to colour a little at the edges. Don't rush this step, you are looking for gentle caramelisation, not burning. Add the garlic, bacon and chorizo and fry until the meat starts to crisp a little.

Stir through the drained beans, and add the bay leaves and smoked paprika. Add enough cold water to cover the beans by a good few centimetres and bring up to a steady boil. Boil, uncovered, for 10 minutes this is important to ensure the beans are properly cooked. Turn the heat down and continue to simmer for 45 minutes. Add the peppers and continue cooking until the beans are soft this will take another 30–45 minutes depending on your beans. Keep an eye on them, stirring regularly to prevent them sticking. Throw in a few splashes of cold water from time to time if they are looking a little dry.

Once the beans are soft and tender, season to taste with salt and freshly ground black pepper. Serve in deep bowls, scattered with the herbs and topped with a dollop of soured cream and orange wedges for squeezing over the beans.

Not suitable for freezing.

Clams with white beans and saffron

This recipe comes from the coast of Asturias, the rural region of northern Spain where my father lives. It is really simple to make and the combination of beans and clams is quite delicious. Flageolet beans can be quite hard to find dried, and haricot beans make a fine substitution if you cannot get hold of them.

Serves 4–6 | Takes 10 minutes to make, approximately 1$\frac{1}{2}$ hours to cook

300g dried flageolet or haricot
  beans, soaked overnight in
  plenty of cold water, drained
  and rinsed
1 large onion, thickly sliced
2 bay leaves
2 sprigs of fresh thyme
4 tbsp olive oil
1 tsp salt
1kg fresh clams
4 large garlic cloves, crushed
175ml dry white wine
bunch of fresh flat-leaf parsley,
  roughly chopped
large pinch of saffron threads
pinch of coarse sea salt
salt and freshly ground black
  pepper
extra virgin olive oil, to serve

Place the beans in a large pan with the onion, herbs and enough cold water to just cover them completely. Bring the beans to the boil, skimming off any scum that collects on the surface and boil for 10 minutes. Reduce the heat to a steady simmer and cook for an hour, adding a little cold water every now and then to make sure the beans just stay covered.

After an hour, add 2 tablespoons of the olive oil and 1 teaspoon of salt and continue to cook until the beans are tender. This may take another 10–20 minutes depending on your beans so keep checking them as you don't want them to disintegrate.

Once the beans are nearly ready you can cook the clams. Firstly rinse them under plenty of cold running water and discard any that are not properly closed.

Heat the remaining olive oil in a large saucepan with a lid. Add the garlic and fry very gently until it just begins to colour. As soon as the garlic begins to turn golden quickly add the wine and half the chopped parsley and bring to the boil. When the wine is boiling, throw in the closed clams and cover the pan. Cook for a few minutes, shaking the pan occasionally, until the clams are open. Strain them, reserving the cooking liquor, and discard any that have refused to open.

Grind the saffron threads in a pestle and mortar with the coarse sea salt and tip into the beans. Add the clams and their strained cooking liquor, stir well and check the seasoning.

Serve in bowls sprinkled with the remaining parsley and a generous glug of extra virgin olive oil.

Not suitable for freezing.

Split pea and golden beetroot hotpot with crispy fried onions

Roasting the beetroot for this simple warming hotpot really intensifies their flavour. Golden beetroot and yellow split peas give this dish a lovely soothing autumn-like colour. You could of course use red beetroot but beware, the stew (and possibly your fingers!) will take on a rather more vivid hue.

Serves 4–6 | Takes 25 minutes to make, 45 minutes to cook

250g split peas, soaked for 4–6 hours in plenty of cold water, drained and rinsed
500–600g golden beetroot (unpeeled weight), peeled and chopped into chunks
4 tbsp olive oil
small bunch of fresh thyme
3 tsp coriander seeds
3 cloves garlic, sliced
1.5 litre vegetable stock
salt and freshly ground black pepper

For the crispy fried onions
2 large onions, finely sliced
vegetable oil, for deep frying

Preheat the oven to 180°C/gas 4.

In a roasting tin toss the beetroot with half the olive oil and thyme. Season generously with salt and freshly ground black pepper. Roast for 25 minutes after which time the beetroot will be turning a deep crisp brown at the edges but it won't be cooked through.

Whilst the beetroot are roasting, dry-fry the coriander seeds in a flameproof casserole. Just as they began to release their aroma scoop them out, and grind them roughly using a pestle and mortar.

Add the remaining olive oil to the casserole and fry the sliced garlic for a couple of minutes until it just begins to colour. Add the drained split peas and the stock and bring up to a steady boil. Boil for 10 minutes before turning the heat down and covering with a lid and simmer steadily until the beetroot are ready.

Once the beetroot have roasted add them to the peas, along with any roasting juices and the ground coriander seeds, and continue cooking. The stew is ready when the split peas are very soft but not completely disintegrating and the beetroot is very tender, this should take around 45 minutes.

Whilst the stew is simmering make the crispy fried onions by heating the vegetable oil in a large frying pan or wok. Once the oil is smoking, carefully add the sliced onions and fry until golden brown and crisp. Use a slotted spoon to remove the onions from the oil and drain on kitchen paper. Set aside.

Taste the stew to check the seasoning and adjust if necessary. Serve in bowls with a generous scattering of onions on top.

Freeze for up to 3 months. Defrost overnight in the fridge before reheating thoroughly. Add a little water or stock if the stew looks a bit dry.

Chestnut, mushroom and savoy cabbage stew

This is another vegetarian stew that meat eaters will love. The chestnuts lend a solid, chewable texture that can often be missing in meat-free dishes. Although you really need no accompaniment to this dish it is delicious with a little mash on the side to soak up the rich buttery juices.

Serves 4–6 | Takes 15 minutes to make, approximately 45 minutes to cook

25g butter
1 tbsp olive oil
12 shallots, peeled and left whole
250g chestnut mushrooms, quartered
2 bay leaves
1 sprig fresh rosemary
200ml red wine
300ml vegetable stock
200g cooked chestnuts, roughly chopped
200g savoy cabbage, finely shredded
1 tbsp plain flour
1 tbsp softened butter
2 tsp Dijon mustard
2 tbsp chopped fresh flat-leaf parsley
salt and freshly ground black pepper

Heat the butter and olive oil in a frying pan and fry the shallots for 5 minutes or so, until they are lightly browned. Add the mushrooms, bay leaves and rosemary and fry for a further 4–5 minutes by which time the mushrooms will be soft.

Add the red wine, stock and chestnuts. Bring to the boil and simmer, uncovered, for 30 minutes until the shallots are soft and the sauce has reduced a little. Add the cabbage, push it into the sauce and cook for a further 5–8 minutes or until it is tender.

Mix the flour and softened butter to form a smooth paste (*beurre manie*).

Once the cabbage is cooked, stir through the beurre manie until it dissolves, and cook at a steady simmer for about 5 minutes until the sauce is thickened.

Stir in the mustard and flat-leaf parsley and season to taste with salt and freshly ground black pepper.

Not suitable for freezing.

Greek chicken and pasta stew

I like to use orzo pasta in this Greek-inspired stew – it's shaped like little rice grains and is great for adding to soups and stews to turn them into a filling meal. There is just a hint of spice that adds subtle warmth to the dish, but more obvious are the unmistakably Mediterranean flavours of thyme, lemon and olives. Sunshine in a bowl for a chilly autumn evening.

Serves 4–6 | Takes 15 minutes to make, approximately 1$\frac{1}{4}$ hours to cook

2 tbsp olive oil
900g skinless, boneless chicken
 thighs
2 onions, sliced
2 cloves garlic, sliced
1 tsp ground cinnamon
1 tsp ground allspice
150ml white wine
400ml chicken stock
400g can chopped tomatoes
1 tbsp tomato purée
2–3 sprigs of fresh thyme
175g orzo pasta (rice shaped
 pasta grains)
handful of kalamata olives
juice of 1 lemon
salt and freshly ground black
 pepper
extra virgin olive oil, to serve

Heat the oil in a heavy-based pan and fry the chicken on both sides until it has a lovely golden crust. Do this in batches if necessary to avoid overcrowding the pan, removing each piece to a plate as it is browned. Set aside.

Lower the heat a little and fry the onions for a few minutes until they are translucent and soft. Add the garlic, cinnamon and allspice and fry for a further minute. Pour in the wine and let it evaporate and reduce, stirring and scraping to release the sticky tasty bits from the bottom of the pan.

Add the chicken stock, chopped tomatoes, tomato purée and thyme. Season well with salt and freshly ground black pepper. Bring up to a steady simmer, cover with a lid and cook for 45 minutes.

Add the pasta and stir well, re-cover the pan and cook for 15 minutes. Then add the olives and lemon juice and simmer, uncovered, for a further 15 minutes, stirring regularly to stop the pasta sticking.

When the pasta is cooked through, taste to check the seasoning and serve in deep bowls drizzled with a little extra olive oil.

Not suitable for freezing.

Cazuela de Vaca

This Chilean beef and vegetable stew is filling and hearty and packed full of healthy vegetables. It is thickened with a little polenta which gives it an unusual and interesting texture. I leave the butternut squash unpeeled as I like the chewy texture of the skin, but feel free to peel it if you prefer.

Serves 4–6 | Takes 15–20 minutes to make, 2–2$^1/_4$ hours to cook

2–3 tbsp vegetable oil
700g braising beef, cut into 5–6cm chunks
2 large onions, sliced
3 cloves garlic, crushed
2 tbsp paprika
2 tsp dried oregano
800ml beef stock
500g butternut squash, cut into 3–4cm chunks
2 medium potatoes cut into 3–4cm chunks
2 carrots, cut into 3cm chunks
2 corn on the cob , each cut into 3 pieces
1 tbsp fine polenta
salt and freshly ground black pepper
large bunch of fresh coriander, roughly chopped, to garnish

Preheat the oven to 160˚C/gas 3.

Heat 2 tablespoons of the oil in a large, flameproof casserole until smoking hot. Quickly sear the meat, a few pieces at a time, on all sides and transfer to a plate.

Add a little more oil if necessary and fry the onion for 5 minutes or so until soft and lightly caramelised. Add the garlic, paprika and oregano and continue to cook for another minute or so.

Return the beef to the casserole and pour over the stock. Bring up to the boil, reduce the heat and cover the casserole and transfer to the oven to cook for an hour.

Add the squash, potatoes, carrots and sweetcorn to the stew. Stir through the polenta and season with salt and black pepper. Re-cover, return to the oven and cook for a further hour or so until the vegetables and beef are tender.

Taste to check the seasoning and serve in deep bowls with the coriander generously scattered over the top.

Not suitable for freezing.

Cuban prawn and rice stew

This is an unusual stew in that it is thickened with a little rice – its almost like a loose risotto – and the combination of lime, cumin and garlic tastes divine.

Serves 4–6 | Takes 15–20 minutes to make, plus marinating, 20–25 minutes to cook

For the marinade
500g raw king prawns, butterflied (see method)
juice of 2 limes
4 cloves garlic, crushed
1 tsp ground cumin
freshly ground black pepper

For the stew
2 tbsp vegetable oil
2 onions, chopped
1 red pepper, deseeded and sliced
175ml white wine
400g can chopped tomatoes
150g long grain rice
1 tsp ground cumin
1 tsp dried oregano
pinch of dried chillies
400ml boiling water
salt

Butterfly the prawns by running a sharp knife along the back, making an incision that goes about half the way through the prawn. They will then open out during cooking which not only looks pretty it helps the marinade soak in really well.

Place the lime, garlic, cumin and a good grind of black pepper in a shallow dish, add the prawns and stir to coat, set aside to marinate in the fridge for 1–2 hours.

When you are ready to make the stew, heat the oil in a heavy-based pan, with a lid. Fry the onion and peppers over a high heat until they are beginning to blacken a little at the edges. This will take about 10 minutes.

Add the remaining ingredients to the pan. Bring to the boil, turn down the heat, cover and simmer for 15 minutes after which time the rice should be very nearly cooked. Stir through the prawns and the marinade and simmer for a further 5 minutes or until the prawns have turned pink all the way through.

Taste to check the seasoning and serve immediately.

Not suitable for freezing.

Butternut squash and red lentils with raita

This stew is loosely based on the beautifully spiced dhals of India. Butternut squash adds a chunky texture that contrasts with the softly melting lentils, while the raita adds a sharpness that lifts the whole dish. Exceptionally soothing and comforting – something for a weeknight when you are feeling cold, frugal and a little out of sorts with the world.

Serves 4–6 | Takes 15–20 minutes to make, 1 hour to cook

1 tbsp coriander seeds
1 tbsp cumin seeds
2–3 tbsp vegetable oil
1 medium butternut squash
    (about 600g), deseeded and cut
    into 3cm pieces
pinch of dried chillies
2 onions, roughly chopped
4 cloves garlic, roughly chopped
5cm piece of fresh root ginger,
    peeled and roughly chopped
250g red lentils
Approximately 600–700ml boiling
    water
salt and freshly ground black
    pepper

For the raita
1 cucumber, peeled and grated
350g plain yogurt
1 clove garlic, crushed
generous handful of fresh
    coriander leaves, roughly
    chopped, to garnish

Start the raita by putting the grated cucumber in a sieve and sprinkling with 1 teaspoon of salt. Set over a bowl for an hour or so to let the water drain out.

Roughly grind the coriander and cumin seeds using a pestle and mortar. Heat 2 tablespoons of the oil in a wide, heavy-based deep frying pan, add the butternut squash and dried chillies and the ground spices. Fry over a medium high heat until the squash colours a little at the edges – this will take at least 5 minutes, maybe a little more.

Resist the temptation to stir too frequently or it won't brown at all.

Purée the onion, garlic and ginger in a food processor, adding a couple of tablespoons of cold water, if necessary, to make a paste. Scrape the purée into the pan and mix it thoroughly with the squash. Fry the purée and squash for a few minutes until the onion begins to soften and look a little translucent. You may need to add a splash more oil if it looks a little dry.

Stir through the lentils and add enough boiling water to cover everything by 2–3cm. Bring up to a simmer, cover loosely with a lid and cook for around 45 minutes or until the lentils are soft and collapsing. You may need to add a little more water towards the end of the cooking time.

Taste to check the seasoning, you will definitely need to add a little salt and maybe some black pepper.

To finish making the raita, stir the drained cucumber through the yogurt. Add the garlic and season with plenty of black pepper. Chill until required.

Serve the stew in deep bowls scattered with the chopped coriander and a generous spoonful of raita.

Freeze the stew for up to 3 months. Defrost overnight in the fridge before reheating thoroughly in the oven at 160°C/gas 3. Reheating gently in the oven prevents the squash breaking up too much on reheating. Raita not suitable for freezing.

Smoked fish chowder with poached eggs

Chowder is often served as a soup for a starter or lunch. This version is a much thicker fish stew packed full of vegetables and topped with a poached egg, it really needs no accompaniment to make it a healthy supper.

Serves 4–6 | Takes 20 minutes to make, 30 minutes to cook

750ml whole milk
750g undyed smoked haddock fillet
1/2 tsp black peppercorns, crushed
2 bay leaves
50g unsalted butter
150g smoked bacon, finely diced
3 sticks celery, finely chopped
2 leeks, washed thoroughly and sliced
2 carrots, chopped
1 clove garlic, crushed
175ml white wine
2 tsp plain flour
4 medium-sized potatoes, peeled and cut into 2cm dice
200g can sweetcorn, drained
generous handful of fresh flat-leaf parsley, roughly chopped
squeeze of lemon juice, to taste
salt

For the poached eggs
4–6 large fresh eggs (allow 1 per person)
1 tsp white wine vinegar

Pour the milk into a wide-based pan and add the fish, you may need to cut it up so it fits in a single layer. Sprinkle over the pepper and tuck in the bay leaves. Bring the milk up to a gentle simmer, cover with a lid or tight-fitting piece of foil, and poach the fish gently for 5–8 minutes. It is cooked when it flakes easily. Gently lift the fish from the pan onto a plate and reserve the poaching liquor.

Melt the butter gently in a large, heavy-based pan and add the bacon, celery, leeks, carrot and garlic and sweat over a low heat for around 10 minutes. The celery and leeks should be translucent and soft but not coloured at all.

Add the white wine to the vegetables and allow it to bubble and reduce by half. Stir in the flour and add the reserved poaching milk, along with the bay leaves and pepper. Stir thoroughly and bring up to the boil. Turn down the heat and add the potatoes and the sweetcorn, cover with a lid and simmer gently until the potatoes are cooked through but not falling apart. This will take around 30 minutes.

Whilst the chowder is simmering flake the fish, discarding the skin and taking care to remove any small bones that may be lurking. Add the fish to the pan just as the potatoes are cooked it only needs warming through. Add the parsley and a squeeze of lemon juice to taste. You may also need to add a little salt depending on how salty the smoked haddock is.

When you are ready to serve, start to poach the eggs by filling a wide-based pan with cold water. Bring up to a rolling boil, add the vinegar and turn the heat down to a gentle simmer. Carefully crack in the eggs, one at a time and allow then to poach undisturbed until they are cooked to your liking.

Serve the chowder in deep bowls, topped with a poached egg.

Not suitable for freezing.

STEWS TO IMPRESS

Stews, by their very nature, are among the simplest of meals to cook. But simplicity doesn't exclude them from the dinner party table, quite the opposite in fact. These are the recipes to turn to when you want to present family or friends with something a little bit special, a little bit different. It is often the addition of alcohol or cream (or both!) that ups the ante in the luxury stakes and gives you a dish that lingers in your memory.

Chicken braised with fennel and brandy

The brandy gives this stew a really rich luxurious taste. I would simply serve this with a mound of buttery tagliatelle and a crisp green salad.

Serves 4–6 | Takes 20 minutes to make, 1½ hours to cook

2 tbsp olive oil
800g chicken thighs, bone in and skin on
25g butter
2 bulbs fennel, cut into 8 pieces through the root
2 onions, finely sliced
3 cloves garlic, sliced
1 tsp fennel seeds
100ml brandy
350ml chicken stock
salt and freshly ground black pepper
tagliatelle and salad, to serve

Heat the oil in a large, heavy-based pan, with a lid, and fry the chicken thighs on both sides until they are golden brown. Do this in several batches if you need to, it is important not to overcrowd the pan. Remove all the chicken to a plate and set aside.

Add the butter to the pan and once it has melted, add the fennel segments and fry on each side until the edges are just begin to caramelise. Then add the onion, garlic and fennel seeds and keep frying for a further couple of minutes. Season with a little salt and freshly ground black pepper.

Pour in the brandy with care – it will splutter and spit a little. Deglaze the pan, scraping all the delicious sticky bits off the bottom. Then return the chicken, and any juices that have collected on the plate, to the pan. Give everything a good stir and bring up to simmering point. Cover loosely with a lid, to allow some evaporation of the sauce, and cook for 1½ hours, by which time the chicken should be beginning to fall off the bone.

Taste to check the seasoning and serve immediately with buttered tagliatelle and salad.

This can be frozen for up to 3 months but the fennel may lose a little of its texture. If you do freeze this stew, defrost overnight in the fridge before reheating thoroughly in the oven at 160°C/ gas 3. Reheating gently in the oven prevents the fennel breaking up too much on reheating.

FISH

Bouillabaisse

This traditional Provençal fish stew is not quick to make but for a special occasion, the results are really worth it. I would urge you to make your own fish stock for this recipe as the flavour will be greatly enhanced.
It is served with a spicy garlic sauce, *rouille*, which you spread on slices of baguette and float on the surface.

Serves 4–6 | Takes 1 hour to make, 45 minutes to cook

2kg mixed white fish (e.g. sea bass, bream, gurnard and monkfish), filleted and bones reserved
12 large shell-on raw tiger prawns, heads cut off and reserved
500g mussels
4 tbsp olive oil
2 leeks, washed thoroughly and finely sliced
2 fennel bulbs, finely sliced
3 cloves garlic, crushed
10–12 new potatoes, scrubbed and sliced
6 plum tomatoes, skinned and chopped
2–3 wide strips of orange peel
2 bay leaves
pinch of saffron threads
2–3 tbsp Pernod
salt and freshly ground black pepper

For the fish stock
fish bones (see above)
prawn heads (see above)
2 sticks celery, sliced
2 carrots, sliced
1 large onion, sliced
handful of fresh parsley (stalks and leaves)
2 bay leaves
6 black peppercorns
1 tsp fennel seeds

For the rouille
1 red pepper
2 cloves garlic, crushed
1 tsp cayenne pepper
125ml good-quality extra virgin olive oil
3 tbsp fresh white breadcrumbs
squeeze of lemon juice, to taste
salt and freshly ground black pepper
handful of fresh flat-leaf parsley, chopped, to garnish
1 baguette, cut into slices, to serve

Begin by making the stock. Put all the ingredients in a large pan with 3 litres of cold water and bring up to the boil. Turn the heat down and simmer for 30 minutes, skimming off any foam that rises to the surface. Strain the liquid into a clean pan and boil rapidly to reduce by a half you are looking for 1–1.2 litres of concentrated stock. Don't be tempted to reduce the stock with the bones still in, they will spoil the flavour if cooked for too long.

Whilst the stock is simmering prepare the mussels by washing them really thoroughly in plenty of cold running water. Discard any that are not closed or do not close with a sharp tap to the shell. Set aside.

Next make the rouille. Preheat the grill to high and grill the red pepper until the skin is blackened. Allow to cool a little before peeling and deseeding. Put the peeled pepper in a blender along with the garlic, and cayenne pepper. Blend to a paste then slowly add the oil with the motor running. Finally add the breadcrumbs to bind the sauce and sharpen to taste with a squeeze of lemon juice, and season with salt and pepper. Set aside.

In a large, heavy-based pan, heat the oil and gently sweat the leek, fennel and garlic for a few minutes until it is beginning to soften and turn translucent, being careful not to let them colour. Add the potatoes, tomatoes, orange peel and bay leaves and cook for a further couple of minutes. Add the saffron threads, pour over the fish stock and Pernod and bring up to a steady simmer. Season with salt and freshly ground black pepper and cover with a tight-fitting lid. Cook for around 15–20 minutes, or until the potatoes are soft but not disintegrating.

Whilst the soup is simmering cut the fish into even-sized pieces of around 5–6cm. When the potatoes are cooked, carefully place the fish on top of the stew, re-cover and cook for 4–5 minutes. Then add the mussels and prawns, turning them gently in the stock but trying not to break up the fish too much. Re-cover and cook for a further 4–5 minutes by which time the fish will be cooked and the mussels will have opened.

Taste the stew to check the seasoning and serve with the parsley scattered over the top and the bowl of rouille and sliced baguette on the side.

Not suitable for freezing.

Wild mushroom stew with ricotta dumplings

I am not going to pretend that these Italian style dumplings are the easiest thing to make – they can be fiddly little blighters! But the result is worth it, light-as-air dumplings floating on a delicious stew of mushrooms heady with garlic and wine.

Serves 4–6 | Takes 30 minutes to make, 25 minutes to cook

25g dried wild porcini mushrooms
250ml boiling water
50g unsalted butter
3 cloves garlic, sliced
750g fresh mixed mushrooms, torn into even-sized pieces
250ml white wine
handful of fresh flat-leaf parsley, chopped

For the dumplings
250g spinach
250g ricotta cheese
50g Parmesan cheese, finely grated
1 bunch fresh basil, leaves roughly torn
2 eggs
125g plain flour, plus extra for dusting
salt and freshly ground black pepper
grated Parmesan cheese, to serve

Place the porcini mushrooms in bowl, pour over the 250ml boiling water and set aside to soak.

Next, make the dumplings (they will happily rest in the fridge for up to a few hours), so you get the fiddly bit out of the way long before your guests arrive! Wash the spinach thoroughly in cold running water and transfer to a large pan with a lid. Wilt over a medium heat for a few minutes until it has completely collapsed, drain and squeeze out as much water as possible, then chop finely. Add to a large bowl along with the ricotta, Parmesan and torn basil leaves and season really generously with salt and freshly ground black pepper. Crack in the eggs and sieve in the flour and mix together thoroughly but as lightly and gently as possible. It is important not to over-mix the dough or the dumplings will lose their light texture.

Sprinkle a light dusting of flour onto a baking sheet, and over your hands, and make the dumplings by forming generous teaspoons of the dough into balls in the palm of your hands. As you make each dumpling lay it gently onto the floured tray. If your hands get sticky with mixture, as they surely will, stop, rinse them well in cold water, dry thoroughly and start again. Cover the dumplings loosely with clingfilm and refrigerate.

Start the stew by melting the butter in a deep, wide frying pan and gently sweating the garlic for a few minutes, taking care not to burn it. Add the torn mushrooms and cook gently until soft - about 10 minutes. Pour in the porcini and their soaking water, being careful to leave the last little bit of water behind as it may contain some unwelcome grit. Add the wine and parsley, cover and stew gently for 10 minutes until the mushrooms are tender and the sauce has reduced a little.

Meanwhile, bring a large pan of salted water to the boil. Gently add the dumplings, in batches, to the boiling water and poach until they float to the surface. Remove with a slotted spoon and keep warm on a plate covered with foil. Taste and season the mushrooms with a little salt and pepper and serve in bowls with the dumplings resting on top. Scatter with Parmesan to serve.

Not suitable for freezing.

Chicken braised with vermouth, pine nuts and raisins

Subtly spiced with cinnamon and rich with pine nuts, this exotic tasting stew is delicious served with plenty of couscous to soak up the sweet juices. A bowl of peppery rocket and watercress salad would be a great accompaniment alongside.

Serves 4–6 | Takes 20 minutes to make, 2 hours to cook

150ml red or white vermouth
150g raisins
2 tbsp plain flour
2 tbsp olive oil
900g chicken legs
2 onions, sliced
3 cloves garlic, sliced
100g toasted pine nuts
1 tsp ground cinnamon
300ml chicken stock
salt and freshly ground black
** pepper**
generous handful of fresh flat-leaf
** parsley, roughly chopped, to**
** garnish**
couscous and rocket and
** watercress salad, to serve**

In a small bowl, pour the vermouth over the raisins and set aside to soak for 20 minutes.

Preheat the oven to 160°C/gas 3.

Season the flour with salt and freshly ground black pepper. Coat the chicken legs in the seasoned flour.

Heat the oil in a large, flameproof casserole and fry the chicken pieces until golden on both sides. You may need to do this in several batches to avoid overcrowding the casserole.

Return all the browned chicken to the casserole, along with the onion, garlic, pine nuts and cinnamon and fry gently for a few minutes. Pour in the raisins and vermouth and add the chicken stock and bring up to a steady simmer. Cover and cook in the oven for 2 hours.

Remove from the oven, scatter over the parsley and serve with couscous and rocket and watercress salad.

Freeze for up to 3 months. Defrost overnight in the fridge before reheating thoroughly. Add a little water or stock if the stew looks a bit dry.

Pork with prunes, cream and Marsala

The combination of pork, cream and fruit is always a marriage made in heaven, and this dish is no exception. The subtle taste of pork tenderloin is really enhanced by the aromatic Marsala. Serve with wild rice and a strong green vegetable such as purple sprouting broccoli. I find that rich cream sauces like this always benefit from something darkly ferrous served alongside.

Serves 4–6 | Takes 15 minutes to make, plus soaking, 1–1$^1/_4$ hours to cook

150g prunes
150ml Marsala
800g pork tenderloin, cut into 1cm thick slices
1 tbsp olive oil
25g unsalted butter
8–10 shallots, peeled and sliced
2 cloves garlic, finely sliced
2 tbsp roughly chopped fresh oregano
350ml chicken stock
150ml double cream
lemon juice, to taste
salt and freshly ground black pepper
wild rice and green vegetables, to serve

Soak the prunes in the Marsala for a couple of hours. If you don't have time to do this, gently warm the Marsala in a pan with the prunes for a few minutes to allow them to become plump with the wine.

Lay the slices of tenderloin on a plate and season well with salt and black pepper on both sides.

Heat the oil and butter in a heavy-based pan, with a lid, and when the butter begins to foam brown the meat, a few pieces at a time, on both sides. As each piece browns, transfer to a plate and set aside.

Lower the heat a little and add the shallots, garlic and oregano to the pan. Sweat gently for a few minutes before adding the prunes and Marsala. Reduce and burn off the alcohol, taking the time to scrape at the bottom of the pan to release any delicious sticky caramelised bits. Return the meat to the pan and pour over the stock. Bring to a gentle simmer, cover with the lid and cook for around 1 hour or until the pork is really tender.

Carefully remove the pork to a serving dish and keep warm by covering tightly in foil. Increase the heat on the hob to bring the sauce to a simmer, add the double cream and allow it to reduce and thicken to the desired consistency. Add a squeeze of lemon juice to sharpen the sauce to your liking. Taste to check the seasoning and add a little more salt and pepper if necessary. Pour the sauce over the meat and serve immediately with wild rice and your choice of green vegetable.

Freeze for up to 3 months. Defrost overnight in the fridge before reheating thoroughly in the oven at 160°C/gas 3. Reheating gently in the oven ensures the prunes do not break up too much. You may need to add a little water if it is looking a touch dry.

Pollo al ajillo

Don't be put off by the sheer quantity of garlic in this traditional Spanish garlic and white wine chicken recipe! The slow braising really mellows it out, giving you an almost roasted flavour. I like to eat this with lots of crusty bread to mop up the delicious sauce and a sharp green palate-cleansing salad.

Serves 4–6 | Takes 15–20 minutes to make, plus overnight marinating, 1½ hours to cook

1kg chicken legs
300ml white wine
100ml extra virgin olive oil
3 whole heads garlic, unpeeled and halved horizontally
3–4 sprigs of fresh thyme
2 tbsp olive oil
200ml chicken stock
salt and freshly ground black pepper
generous handful of fresh flat-leaf parsley, roughly chopped, to garnish
crusty bread and green salad, to serve

Place the chicken legs in a large non-metallic bowl and pour over the white wine and extra virgin olive oil. Add the garlic and thyme and season well with salt and black pepper. Stir thoroughly, cover with cling film and marinate in the fridge overnight.

When you are ready to begin cooking, preheat the oven to 180°C/gas 4.

Remove the chicken from the marinade, scraping off and reserving as much of the marinade as possible. Lay the chicken on a plate and pat dry with kitchen paper.

Heat the olive oil in a large, flameproof casserole until smoking hot. Fry the chicken pieces on both sides until crisp and golden.

Add the reserved marinade, along with the garlic and thyme, and stock to the casserole. Bring up to the boil and cover with a lid. Transfer to the oven and cook for 1½ hours or until the chicken is so tender it is falling off the bone.

Carefully remove the chicken to a serving dish, along with the garlic cloves, and keep warm. Place the casserole over a high heat and boil the sauce really rapidly, whisking to emulsify the oil with the wine. Once the sauce is glossy and reduced, pour it over the chicken and garnish with the flat-leaf parsley. Serve with the bread and salad.

Not suitable for freezing.

Venison and chestnut casserole

For me this dish is autumn on a plate, exactly the kind of thing you want to eat as the clocks turn back and the first frosts are in the air. I absolutely have to have rich creamy mash with this, but rice would be a excellent alternative if you were feeling more virtuous.

Serves 4–6 | Takes 10–15 minutes to make, $1\frac{1}{2}$–2 hours to cook

2 tbsp plain flour
900g shoulder of venison, diced into 3cm chunks
2 tbsp oil
3 red onions, sliced
3 cloves garlic, crushed
300ml red wine
300ml beef stock
200g cooked chestnuts, roughly cut
2 tbsp redcurrant jelly
2 bay leaves
2 sprigs of fresh rosemary
salt and freshly ground black pepper
mashed potato or rice, to serve

Season the flour with salt and freshly ground black pepper. Toss the venison in the seasoned flour, ensuring each piece is well coated.

Heat the oil in a heavy-based pan, with a lid, and quickly brown the meat a few pieces at time. Transfer each piece to a plate as it is done and set aside.

Add a splash more oil to the pan if necessary and fry the onions for a few minutes until they start to soften. Add the garlic and cook for a further minute before returning all the meat and juices to the pan. Pour in the wine and stock and stir through the chestnuts and redcurrant jelly. Tuck the herbs in amongst the meat and bring gently up to a simmer. Cover with a tight-fitting lid and cook over the lowest heat for $1\frac{1}{2}$–2 hours by which time the venison should be really very tender.

Taste to check the seasoning and serve with mash or rice and a vegetable of your choice.

Freeze for up to 3 months. Defrost overnight in the fridge before reheating thoroughly.

Pork with pancetta, sage and lemon

This stew has an Italian feel to it, which to my mind makes long ribbons of pasta the ideal accompaniment. The cubes of pork are studded with little pinches of zesty stuffing which helps to flavour and tenderise the meat from the inside. If you were really short on time you could simply mix the stuffing ingredients through the cubes of pork as a marinade rather than stuffing them.

Serves 4–6 | Takes 25 minutes to make, plus marinating, 2 hours to cook

For the stuffing
200g diced pancetta, ideally smoked
zest of 2 lemons
small bunch of fresh sage, finely chopped
2–3 fat cloves garlic, crushed
freshly ground black pepper

For the stew
1kg boneless pork shoulder, cut into 4cm cubes
1 tbsp olive oil
1 onion, finely diced
1 carrot, finely diced
1 stick celery, finely diced
400g can chopped tomatoes
500ml chicken stock
175ml red wine
salt
tagliatelle or pappadelle, to serve

In a large, heavy-based pan, with a lid, fry the pancetta gently until the fat runs and it is just starting to crisp. Remove to a small bowl (set the pan aside for later) and allow to cool for a few minutes before mixing in the lemon zest, sage, garlic and a generous grind of black pepper. Make deep slits into each cube of pork and stuff little pinches of the pancetta and lemon mixture inside. Leave the pork to marinate for an hour or so to let the stuffing flavours infuse the meat.

When the pork has finished marinating begin the stew by adding the oil to the pan the pancetta was cooked in. Sear the cubes of meat a few at a time over a high heat until they are nicely brown on all sides. As each piece is browned remove to a plate and set aside.

Once all the meat has been seared return it all to the pan, lower the heat a little and add the onion, carrot and celery. Allow the vegetables to soften for a few minutes before pouring in the tomatoes, chicken stock and wine. Add the crisp pancetta and season with a little salt and freshly ground black pepper and bring up to a steady simmer. Cover with a lid and simmer very gently for around 2 hours or until the pork is really tender.

Taste and adjust the seasoning and serve with the pasta.

Not suitable for freezing.

Spiced beef with prunes, apricots and pecans

I think of this as a good festive entertaining stew as it is packed full of the fruits, nuts, spices and port we have at home during the Christmas season. Serve with savoy cabbage and buttery mashed potatoes.

Serves 4–6 | Takes 20 minutes to make, plus marinating, 2$\frac{1}{2}$ hours to cook

150g dried prunes
150g dried apricots
150ml port
2 tsp ground coriander
1 tsp ground cinnamon
1 tsp ground mace
$\frac{1}{2}$ tsp cayenne pepper
2 tbsp plain flour
1kg skirt beef, cut into 2cm strips
2–3 tbsp olive oil
2 onions, sliced
3cm piece fresh root ginger, peeled and finely grated
3 cloves garlic, crushed
300ml beef stock
300ml red wine
salt and freshly ground black pepper

For the spiced nuts
1 tbsp olive oil
125g pecans
pinch of ground cinnamon
savoy cabbage and mashed potatoes, to serve

In a small bowl, soak the prunes and apricots in the port. Ideally leave for a few hours to infuse. If you are short of time you can put the bowl in the oven at 140°C/gas 1 for 20–30 minutes to speed up the process.

In a large bowl mix the dry spices and flour together, add the meat, mixing well so each piece is evenly coated.

Heat 2 tablespoons of the oil in a large, heavy-based pan, with a lid, and fry the pieces of meat a few at a time to quickly brown them on all sides. As the meat is browned remove to a plate and continue until all the beef is done. Set aside.

Lower the heat, add a splash more oil if necessary and fry the onions until they are soft and beginning to colour. Add the ginger and garlic and fry for another couple of minutes before returning the meat and any juices to the pan. Pour in the beef stock and red wine and bring up to a gentle simmer. Add a little salt and freshly ground black pepper, cover with a lid and reduce the heat to as low as possible. Cook very gently for 2 hours.

Stir through the port-soaked prunes and apricots and cook for a further 30 minutes. If the sauce is still quite thin at this stage remove the lid and allow it to thicken gently.

Whilst the stew is cooking prepare the spiced pecans, heat the oil over a medium heat and add the nuts and cinnamon, fry them for a couple of minutes.

Check the seasoning and serve the stew with the spiced nuts scattered over the top, accompanied by the cabbage and mash.

Freeze the stew for up to 3 months. Defrost overnight in the fridge before reheating thoroughly in the oven at 160°C/gas 3. Reheating gently in the oven prevents the dried fruit breaking up too much on reheating. Spiced pecans not suitable for freezing.

Beef stifado with tzatziki

Stifado is a classic Greek stew that is made a little more special here with the addition of a creamy tzatziki which melts gently over the top. I would serve this with crunchy rosemary and garlic roast potatoes and a green salad.

Serves 4–6 | Takes 30 minutes to make, 2 hours to cook

For the stifado
2–3 tbsp olive oil
800g braising beef, cut into 3cm chunks
500g shallots, peeled but left whole
3 cloves garlic, crushed
2 tsp dried oregano
1 tsp ground allspice
$^1/_2$ tsp ground nutmeg
$^1/_2$ tsp ground cinnamon
350ml passata
150ml beef stock or water
2 tbsp red wine vinegar
2 strips of orange peel

For the tzatziki
400ml Greek yogurt
1 cucumber, peeled and grated
2 cloves garlic, crushed
juice of $^1/_2$ lemon
salt and freshly ground black pepper

crunchy rosemary and garlic roast potatoes and green salad, to serve

Begin the stifado by heating 2 tablespoons of the oil in a heavy-based pan, with a lid, and browning the beef in batches. As each piece of beef is browned, transfer it to a plate and set aside.

Once all the beef has been browned add a little more oil to the pan if necessary. Fry the shallots for a few minutes until they are starting to caramelise and soften slightly. Return the beef to the pan along with the garlic, oregano and spices.

Pour in the passata, stock or water and red wine vinegar and add the strips of orange peel. Bring up to a steady simmer, cover with a lid, reduce the heat to as low as possible and cook very gently for around 2 hours or until the beef is so tender it's almost falling apart.

Whilst the beef is cooking prepare the tzatziki. Place a colander over a bowl and add the grated cucumber. Sprinkle over 1 teaspoon of salt and mix well. Leave to rest for 10 minutes then squeeze out as much water as possible. Stir the drained cucumber through the yogurt and add the garlic, lemon juice and black pepper to taste. Set aside in the fridge.

Serve the stifado with a generous spoonful of tzatziki on top and the roast potatoes and salad.

Rosemary and garlic roast potatoes
To make the rosemary and garlic roast potatoes, scrub 1kg new potatoes and cut in half. Toss them in 4–5 tablespoons of olive oil and 1 heaped teaspoon of crunchy sea salt. Tip into a roasting pan and add 4 bruised unpeeled cloves of garlic and a few sprigs of rosemary. Roast in a hot oven for around 30 minutes or until they are crisp on the outside and cooked through.

Freeze the stew for up to 3 months. Defrost overnight in the fridge before reheating thoroughly. Tzatziki not suitable for freezing.

Venison with juniper and white wine

Venison is traditionally paired with juniper berries; it's just one of those partnerships that works really well. Although rich in taste, venison is a really lean and healthy meat so I feel it's perfectly acceptable to serve this with gloriously creamy dauphinoise potatoes. And I'd most likely follow it with a sharply dressed green salad.

Serves 4–6 | Takes 20 minutes to make, plus overnight marinating, 2 hours to cook

10 juniper berries
1kg venison (shoulder or flank), cut into 3cm cubes
750ml bottle dry white wine
10 black peppercorns, roughly crushed
2–3 sprigs of fresh thyme
2 cloves garlic, crushed
2–3 tbsp olive oil
6 shallots, peeled and quartered
1 tbsp plain flour
salt and freshly ground black pepper
dauphinoise potatoes, to serve

Bruise the juniper berries using a pestle and mortar. In a large non-metallic bowl, marinate the venison in the wine, juniper berries, peppercorns, thyme and garlic. Cover with clingfilm and leave in the fridge overnight if possible, or for at least 3 hours.

When you are ready to begin the stew, lift the meat out of the marinade and pat dry with kitchen paper. Reserve the marinade.

Heat 2 tablespoons of the oil in a large, heavy-based pan and brown the venison in batches, transferring each piece to a plate as it is done. Add a splash more oil if necessary and fry the shallots until they are colouring a little at the edges. Sprinkle over the flour and mix thoroughly.

Return the venison to the pan, along with the reserved marinade and bring up to a steady simmer. Reduce the heat, cover with a lid or tightly-fitting piece of foil and cook gently for about 2 hours or until the venison is tender.

Taste carefully and season with salt and possibly a little more black pepper. Serve with the dauphinoise potatoes.

Freeze for up to 3 months. Defrost overnight in the fridge before reheating thoroughly, adding a splash more water if it looks a little dry.

Lamb shanks with red wine and balsamic vinegar

The sheer quantity of red wine and balsamic vinegar in this dish give it a really rich and intense flavour ideally suited to a winter dinner party. This is great served with mashed potato into which you have stirred a handful each of chopped fresh flat-leaf parsley and torn fresh basil leaves.

Serves 4–6 | Takes 20 minutes to make, 2$\frac{1}{2}$ hours to cook

2 tbsp plain flour
4–6 lamb shanks
2–3 tbsp olive oil
4 red onions, cut into wedges through the root
3 cloves garlic, crushed
1 tbsp fresh rosemary leaves
375ml red wine
150ml balsamic vinegar
salt and freshly ground black pepper
herby mashed potato (see introduction), to serve

Season the flour with salt and freshly ground black pepper. On a large plate dust the lamb shanks with the seasoned flour and toss to coat all over.

Heat 2 tablespoons of the olive oil in a heavy-based pan, with a lid, and brown the lamb shanks on all sides. This will take a good few minutes so don't rush it as the flavour will be greatly improved if the shanks are well browned. Remove to a plate and set aside.

Add a little more oil to the pan if necessary and add the onions and allow to soften and colour a little at the edges. Then add the garlic and rosemary cook for just a minute before returning the lamb shanks to the pan and pouring over the red wine and balsamic vinegar. Bring up to a simmer, cover with a lid and cook very slowly for 2–2$\frac{1}{2}$ hours. You want the lamb to be so soft it is coming away from the bone. Turn the shanks every now and then to baste them in the juices.

Check the seasoning and adjust if necessary and serve with the herby mash.

Freeze for up to 3 months. Defrost overnight in the fridge before reheating thoroughly in the oven at 160°C/gas 3. Reheating gently in the oven ensures the lamb shanks heat evenly. You may need to add a splash of water if the dish looks a little dry.

Chicken braised with red wine, garlic and fresh figs

This dish makes the most of the gorgeous Turkish black figs that come into the shops during September. Weather permitting, it would make the perfect end-of-summer celebratory meal eaten with your loved ones under the stars. Plenty of wine to drink is, of course, essential to keep you warm from the inside out!

Serves 4–6 | Takes 15 minutes to make, 2 hours to cook

2 tbsp olive oil
900g chicken thighs, skin on and
   bone in
2 onions, thinly sliced
2–3 sprigs of fresh rosemary
2 bay leaves
6 cloves garlic, peeled and bruised
300ml red wine
300ml chicken stock
6 fresh figs, halved
zest of 1 lemon
salt and freshly ground black
   pepper
bunch of fresh flat-leaf parsley,
   roughly chopped, to garnish
warm, crusty bread, to serve

Preheat the oven to 160°C/gas 3.

In a wide, ovenproof frying pan or casserole heat the oil until it is just smoking – ideally you need the chicken thighs to fit snugly in a single layer. Add the chicken thighs, skin side down and fry until really crisp and golden. Turn over and fry on the other side, then add the onions and continue to fry until they soften and begin to colour at the edges.

Turn the heat down and tuck the rosemary, bay leaves and garlic in amongst the chicken. Pour over the wine and stock and season with salt and plenty of freshly ground black pepper. Bring to a gentle simmer, cover the pan with a lid or tightly-fitting piece of foil. Transfer to the oven and cook for $1\frac{1}{2}$ hours.

Press a little lemon zest onto the cut surface of each fig. Remove the stew from the oven, and squeeze the figs into the gaps between the chicken. Return to the oven, uncovered, for 20–30 minutes or until the figs are really soft and the chicken tender.

Scatter generously with the flat-leaf parsley and serve with lots of warm crusty bread to soak up the rich, sweet juices.

Not suitable for freezing.

Rabbit with red wine and herbs

Rabbit is a cheap and underused game meat that is well worth sourcing from your butcher. It ticks all the right boxes in terms of animal welfare and is really lean, healthy and packed full of protein. Here it is slowly braised in red wine and herbs to make a deliciously different stew. I like to serve this with a peppery watercress salad and buttered pasta.

Serves 4–6 | Takes 15 minutes to make, 2–2$\frac{1}{2}$ hours to cook

**1 tbsp plain flour
2 rabbits, skinned and each
    jointed into 6 pieces
2 tbsp olive oil
500ml red wine
125ml red wine vinegar
2 tbsp brown sugar
8 fat cloves garlic, peeled and
    bruised
12 fresh sage leaves, roughly
    chopped
2 sprigs of fresh rosemary
salt and freshly ground black
    pepper
watercress salad and buttered
    pasta, to serve**

Season the flour with salt and freshly ground black pepper. Lay the jointed rabbit on a plate and sprinkle with the seasoned flour, turning each piece to ensure it is evenly coated.

Heat the oil in a large, wide pan, with a lid, and fry the rabbit pieces until they are browned all over. Do this in batches to ensure it browns evenly and quickly.

Return all the meat to the pan, pour over the wine and wine vinegar and add the sugar, garlic and herbs. Bring up to a gentle simmer, cover with a lid and cook over a low heat for 2–2$\frac{1}{2}$ hours, or until the rabbit is tender and falling off the bone. Remove the lid about 30 minutes before the end of cooking to let the sauce reduce and thicken.

Taste to check the seasoning and serve spooned over buttered pasta with the salad on the side.

Freeze for up to 3 months. Defrost overnight in the fridge before reheating thoroughly in the oven at 160°C/gas 3. Reheating gently in the oven ensures the rabbit heats evenly, you may need to add a little water or stock if it is looking dry.

Pheasant with capers and prosciutto

If you have never cooked pheasant before, this stew is a great introduction. It is rich with Mediterranean flavours that will bring some welcome sunshine to your autumn entertaining. I like to eat this with fettuccine tossed in my very best olive oil and generously seasoned with black pepper.

Serves 4–6 | Takes 15–20 minutes to make, 1½ hours to cook

2 tbsp olive oil
2 pheasants, each jointed into
    4 pieces
100g prosciutto, finely chopped
6 shallots, peeled and quartered
3 cloves garlic, sliced
6 tomatoes, quartered
400ml chicken stock
175ml white wine
2 tbsp capers in salt or brine,
    rinsed
handful of fresh flat-leaf parsley,
    roughly chopped
handful of fresh basil, roughly
    chopped
salt and freshly ground black
    pepper
fettuccine tossed in olive oil and
    black pepper, to serve

In a wide, heavy-based pan, heat the oil until smoking hot and quickly sear the pheasant pieces until they are golden brown all over. Do this in two or three batches and transfer to a plate to rest.

Reduce the heat a little and gently fry the prosciutto and shallots until they begin to caramelise. Avoid rushing this step if you fry over too high a heat they will burn rather than caramelise it will take a good few minutes. Add the garlic and fry for a further minute before returning the pheasant pieces to the pan.

Pour in the chopped tomatoes, followed by the stock and white wine and a little salt and black pepper. Bring slowly up to a gentle simmer, cover with a tightly-fitting lid and cook gently for about 1 hour.

Stir through the capers and simmer for another 20–30 minutes after which the pheasant should be falling away from the bone. Leave the lid off for this final stage of cooking to allow the sauce to thicken gently.

Remove from the heat, stir through the parsley and basil and taste to check the seasoning. Serve with the fettuccine tossed in olive oil and black pepper.

Freeze for up to 3 months. Defrost overnight in the fridge before reheating thoroughly in the oven at 160°C/gas 3. Reheating gently in the oven ensures the pheasant heats evenly, you may need to add a little water or stock if it is looking dry.

Pork braised in spiced milk

A wonderful stew based on a traditional dish from central Italy. It might sound like a slightly odd thing to cook meat in milk but this is deliciously aromatic and comforting. The mildly spiced creamy flavours remind me a little of one of my all-time favourite things to eat – bread sauce! It is a rich dish so is best served with plain rice and something deeply green, like wilted spinach or purple sprouting broccoli.

Serves 4–6 | Takes 10–15 minutes to make, $2^{1}/_{2}$ hours to cook

2 tbsp olive oil
25g unsalted butter
4–6 pork shoulder steaks, allow 1 per person
500ml whole milk
4 cloves, slightly bruised with the flat of a knife
6 black peppercorns
pinch of ground cinnamon
sprig of fresh rosemary
1 bay leaf
4 garlic cloves, peeled and bruised
salt and freshly ground black pepper
rice and green vegetables, to serve

Preheat the oven to 140°C/gas 1.

In a heavy, flameproof casserole heat the oil and melt the butter. Once the butter begins to foam slightly add the pork steaks and seal well on both sides. You are looking for meat that is a rich golden colour so don't be tempted to keep turning it over as this will cool the pan and the meat will simply sweat. It will take a good few minutes on each side, be patient.

Pour the milk slowly over the browned pork and add the spices, herbs and garlic. Add a little salt and freshly ground black pepper and turn the meat over a few times to mix the aromatics with the milk. Cover with a lid, bring to a steady low simmer and transfer to the oven to cook gently for about $2^{1}/_{2}$ hours or until the meat is very tender. Turn the pork steaks over a couple of times during cooking to baste them in the spiced milk.

At the end of cooking you should be left with a fairly thick, rich sauce and the milk will have separated a little into caramelised golden nuggets. Some may find this a little off-putting – 1 tablespoon of boiling water whisked in at this stage will bring the sauce back to a slightly more even consistency. But it will taste great either way. You can remove the spices and herbs before serving if you wish, or let your guests find them hidden in the sauce. Check and adjust the seasoning and serve the steaks with the sauce poured over, accompanied by the rice and vegetables.

Not suitable for freezing.

Veal with white wine and gremolata

This has all the same ingredients and flavours as the Italian classic, *Osso Bucco Milanese*. But I use welfare-friendly rose veal steak instead of the traditional bone-in veal shin, simply because I find it easier to source from my local butcher. British rose veal has a slightly pink flesh, hence the name, and is produced from calves that are allowed plenty of freedom to move around and eat a balanced diet. This rich and delicious stew is topped with punchy gremolata and is great served with crisp sauté potatoes scattered with a little finely grated Parmesan cheese.

Serves 4–6 | Takes 25 minutes to make, 1 hour to cook

2 tbsp plain flour
1 tbsp dried oregano
800g rose veal steak, diced into 3cm pieces
1 tbsp olive oil
50g unsalted butter
2 medium leeks, washed thoroughly, sliced lengthways and finely diced
2 carrots, finely diced
2 sticks celery, finely diced
2 cloves garlic, crushed
400ml white wine
400ml chicken stock
salt and freshly ground black pepper

For the gremolata
zest of 2 lemons
generous handful of fresh flat-leaf parsley, finely chopped
2 garlic cloves, finely chopped
sauté potatoes sprinkled with grated Parmesan cheese, to serve

On a large plate, season the flour generously with salt, black pepper and the dried oregano. Roll the diced veal in the flour making sure each piece is evenly coated.

Heat the oil and butter in a large, heavy-based pan, with a lid. When the butter begins to foam add half the veal and quickly brown it all over. Remove it to a plate and brown the other half of the veal, also removing it to a plate.

Add the leeks, carrots, celery and garlic to the pan and fry for a couple of minutes to soften a little. Pour in the wine and let it bubble steadily until it is really reduced and syrupy. Return the meat to the pan along with the stock and bring everything up to a gentle simmer. Cover with the lid, reduce the heat to as low as possible and simmer for about 1 hour after which the meat should be really tender.

Whilst the stew is cooking make the gremolata by combining the lemon zest, parsley and garlic in a small bowl. Set aside.

When the stew is ready, taste to check the seasoning and adjust if necessary. Serve immediately with the gremolata sprinkled over the top, accompanied by the sauté potatoes.

Freeze the stew for up to 3 months. Defrost overnight in the fridge before reheating thoroughly. Gremolata not suitable for freezing and is best made just before serving as it will loose its zestiness if it sits around for too long.

Beef with cream and green peppercorns

The inspiration for this dish is the classic creamy pepper sauce served with steak. The idea being that you get the rich luxurious taste without the steak price-tag. Skirt is an underused, but really tasty and economical cut of beef – you may need to order it from your butcher, but the extra effort is worth it. If you can't get skirt, substitute with braising steak. This is really quite a peppery dish so if you or your guests are a little pepper-shy just don't add the black pepper at the beginning. I would serve this stew, perhaps controversially, with thin, crispy chips and a mound of soft English lettuce to mop up the creamy sauce. But mash would be good too.

Serves 4–6 | Takes 15 minutes to make, 2$\frac{1}{2}$ hours to cook

900g piece beef skirt
1 tbsp black peppercorns, roughly crushed
pinch of coarse sea salt
2 tbsp olive oil
3–5 tbsp brandy
2 cloves garlic, crushed
400ml beef stock
125ml double cream
2–3 tbsp green peppercorns in brine, rinsed and bruised
thin, crispy chips and English lettuce or mashed potato, to serve

Preheat the oven to 140°C/gas 1.

Slice the beef skirt into 1–2cm wide strips making sure you cut across the grain of the meat. If you follow the grain you will end up with a stew as tough as old boots! Sprinkle the beef with the crushed black peppercorns and rub in the sea salt.

In a large, heavy, flameproof casserole, with a lid, heat the oil over a high heat until it is just smoking. Fry the beef strips in batches to seal and get a good golden-brown crust, being careful not to overcrowd the pan. As each piece of beef is browned, transfer it to a plate and set aside.

Add the brandy to the casserole with a flourish it will spit and sizzle and deglaze the pan, scraping all the sticky brown tasty bits off the bottom. Return the meat to the pan, along with the crushed garlic and stock. Bring to a gentle simmer and cover with the lid. Cook in the oven for 2–2$\frac{1}{2}$ hours or until the beef is literally falling apart.

Once the meat is meltingly tender remove it with a slotted spoon and set aside on a warm plate to rest. Transfer the casserole to the hob, add the cream and bruised green peppercorns, bring to the boil and reduce to a desired consistency. I like it to be similar to thick double cream, so it coats the meat wonderfully. Return the meat to the pan and taste and adjust the seasoning as necessary. It goes without saying you are unlikely to need extra pepper, but a little more salt may just bring it to life.

Serve the beef and sauce with the chips and lettuce or mashed potato.

Freeze for up to 3 months. Defrost overnight in the fridge before reheating thoroughly.

PORK

Pork with caramelised apples, crème fraîche and wholegrain mustard

This is delicious – sweet, creamy pork with a sharp mustard kick, my idea of eating heaven. I like to eat this with garlicky crushed potatoes and wilted spring greens.

Serves 4–6 | Takes 15–20 minutes to make, 2 hours to cook

1 tbsp olive oil
25g butter
4–6 pork shoulder steaks
3 fat cloves garlic, crushed
500ml dry cider
loose handful of fresh sage leaves
1–2 tbsp wholegrain mustard
4 tbsp full fat crème fraîche
salt and freshly ground black
**   pepper**

For the caramelised apples
25g unsalted butter
1 tbsp caster sugar
2 eating apples, peeled, cored and
**   cut into slices**

garlicky crushed potatoes and
**   wilted spring greens, to serve**

Heat the oil and butter in a large, heavy-based pan, with a lid, and fry the pork steaks on both sides until golden. Add the garlic and fry for a further minute or so, taking care not to burn it or it will give the dish a bitter note.

Pour over the cider and tuck in the sage leaves. Season well with salt and freshly ground black pepper and bring up to a steady simmer. Cover with a lid and cook for around 2 hours, or until the pork is very tender.

Whilst the pork is cooking, make the caramelised apples by melting the butter

in a heavy-based frying pan. Sprinkle in the sugar and allow it to melt. Add the apple slices and fry on both sides until soft and golden. Transfer to a plate and keep warm.

When the pork is tender, carefully transfer to a plate and keep warm. Turn up the heat on the sauce and boil rapidly to reduce and thicken. Once the sauce has thickened, turn off the heat and stir through the mustard and crème fraîche and taste to check the seasoning.

Serve the pork with the sauce poured over and the apple slices on the side, accompanied by the garlicky potatoes and greens.

Garlicky crushed potatoes
To make the garlicky crushed potatoes simply boil peeled and chopped potatoes until they are just tender and drain well. Add a generous knob of butter, a crushed garlic clove and a seasoning of salt and freshly ground black pepper. Stir through until the butter has melted, crushing the potatoes lightly with a fork.

Freeze stew for up to 3 months. Defrost overnight in the fridge before reheating thoroughly in the oven at 160°C/gas 3. Reheating gently in the oven ensures the pork steaks heat evenly, you may need to add a little water or stock if it is looking dry. Caramelized apples not suitable for freezing, so make these just before serving.

Pork with mushrooms, Oloroso sherry and crème fraîche

This pork dish is made really rich with glorious Oloroso sherry and crème fraîche so is best served with simple mashed potatoes and green vegetables – tenderstem broccoli is ideal. When I serve this for a dinner party I like to serve the rest of the bottle of Oloroso as a chilled aperitif with a few roasted almonds – heaven!

Serves 4–6 | Takes 15 minutes to make, 2 hours to cook

2 tbsp olive oil
800g boneless pork shoulder,
  cut into 3cm chunks
1 large onion, sliced
150ml dry Oloroso sherry
3 cloves garlic, crushed
250g chestnut mushrooms,
  quartered
2 tbsp fresh thyme leaves
4 tbsp crème fraîche
salt and freshly ground black
  pepper
mashed potatoes and green
  vegetables, to serve

Heat the oil in a large, wide pan and fry the pork pieces quickly until they are golden brown on all sides. Add the onion and fry until it starts to soften and caramelise slightly. Deglaze the pan with the sherry, being sure to scrape the delicious sticky bits off the bottom of the pan.

Add the garlic, mushrooms and thyme and allow to soften for a few minutes before pouring over 600ml water. Season with salt and freshly ground black pepper and bring up to a steady simmer. Cover with a lid or tight-fitting piece of foil, turn the heat down and simmer gently for around 2 hours or until the pork is really tender and soft.

Using a slotted spoon, remove the pork pieces to a serving dish and cover tightly with foil to keep warm. Bring the sauce up to the boil and reduce a little. Add the crème fraîche and taste to check the seasoning. Pour the sauce over the pork and serve immediately with the mash and vegetables.

Not suitable for freezing.

Quail braised with honey and thyme

There is something special about being served individual birds for your supper, but you could in theory substitute the quail for a large jointed chicken if you prefer or if you can't buy quail. This aromatic braise goes brilliantly with nutty wild rice and a dish of simple wilted spinach.

Serves 4–6 | Takes 15 minutes to make, 1 hour to cook

small bunch of fresh thyme
8 prepared quail (you need 1–2 quail per person – some people will easily eat 2, others will eat 1, so 8 will serve 4–6 people)
1 lemon, cut into 8 slices
4 fat cloves garlic, peeled and halved
2–3 tbsp olive oil
50g unsalted butter
200ml white port or white wine
400ml chicken stock
3 tsp honey, set or clear
salt and freshly ground black pepper
wild rice and wilted spinach, to serve

Preheat the oven to 160°C/gas 3.

Divide the thyme into stems and stuff some thyme inside each quail, along with a piece of lemon and a half clove of garlic. Measure out 2 tablespoons of the olive oil and rub the outside of each bird with a little of this olive oil, season generously with salt and freshly ground black pepper. You can do this ahead of time and leave the quail to rest in the fridge if you like.

Heat half the butter and the remaining olive oil in a flameproof casserole and brown the quail on all sides. Pour in the port and the stock, and stir in the honey. Bring up to a gentle simmer, cover with a lid and transfer to the oven. Cook for about an hour or until the quail are very tender. Turn the quail over once during cooking time to baste them in the juices.

Transfer the casserole back to the hob and carefully remove the quail to a warmed serving dish. Boil the sauce rapidly, uncovered, for about 5 minutes to reduce and concentrate it. Add the remaining butter to the sauce and whisk until syrupy and glossy. This should give you plenty of tasty, thinnish gravy, which is what I like to soak into the rice grains. If you prefer a thicker sauce just keep simmering until the sauce is the desired consistency.

Taste the sauce to check the seasoning and adjust if necessary. Serve the quail with the sauce poured over, and the rice and wilted spinach.

Freeze for up to 3 months. Defrost overnight in the fridge before reheating thoroughly in the oven at 160°C/gas 3. Reheating gently in the oven ensures the quails heat evenly, you may need to add a little water or stock if it is looking dry.

FRAGRANT AND AROMATIC

Every country in the world has their own ways of stewing food – stewing after all is just cooking meat and vegetables in a liquid. Recipes we don't necessarily think of as 'stew' are stewed dishes – the slow cooked curries of India and south-east Asia and the tagines of Morocco are all fragrantly spiced stews. Turn to this chapter when you want your senses awakened, and a little fire and spice in your belly.

Turlu Turlu

This fragrant spiced vegetable stew from Turkey is delicious served with flatbread to soak up the delicious fragrant juices. It makes a brilliant vegetarian main course but is also great with simply grilled chicken or fish.

Serves 4–6 | Takes 20–25 minutes to make, 40 minutes to cook

3 tbsp extra virgin olive oil
1 aubergine, chopped
1 green pepper, chopped
1 red pepper, chopped
1 courgette, sliced
1 onion, sliced
2 carrots, sliced
1 turnip, cut into wedges
3 cloves garlic, thickly sliced
400g can chopped tomatoes
400g can chickpeas, drained and rinsed
2 tsp coriander seeds, lightly crushed
$1/2$ teaspoon allspice berries, lightly crushed
bunch of fresh flat-leaf parsley, roughly chopped
bunch of fresh coriander, roughly chopped
salt and freshly ground black pepper

For the yogurt dressing
250ml Greek yogurt
1 clove garlic, crushed

flatbread, to serve

Heat the olive oil in a wide heavy-based pan, with a lid, (a deep frying pan is ideal) and add the aubergine, green and red peppers, courgette and onion. Fry over a fairly high heat until the vegetables start to colour and caramelise a little at the edges. It is important not to rush this step as it will really enhance the flavour of the finished dish. It may take as much as 15 minutes to get the required colour.

Whilst the vegetables are frying make the yogurt dressing by simply mixing all the ingredients together, season well and set aside.

Once the vegetables are golden, add the carrots, turnip and garlic and fry for a couple more minutes. Pour in the chopped tomatoes, along with the chickpeas, spices and 200ml water. Season with a little salt and pepper. Bring everything up to the boil, turn down the heat and simmer, covered, for around 30 minutes, or until the sauce is thick and rich. Halfway though cooking, remove the lid if the sauce is a little thin.

Turn off the heat, add the chopped herbs and allow to rest for a few minutes to allow the flavours of the herbs to infuse.

Serve hot or warm with a generous dollop of yogurt dressing on top and plenty of flatbread to soak up the juices.

Not suitable for freezing – the peppers and aubergines will not freeze well and will become mushy on reheating.

Trinidad chicken and coconut stew

This sweet stew from Trinidad uses the West Indian technique of browning the meat which is found in many Caribbean dishes, where the meat is fried quickly in hot oil and brown sugar to get a lovely toffee flavour and colour before you add the rest of the ingredients. It is quite a rich dish so is best served with plain steamed or boiled rice.

Serves 4–6 | Takes 20 minutes to make, 1 hour to cook

2 tbsp vegetable oil
1 tbsp brown sugar
8 skinless, boneless chicken
    thighs, cut into 3–4cm pieces
1 onion, chopped
1 green pepper, chopped
2 cloves garlic, crushed
2cm piece of fresh root ginger,
    peeled and diced
200g creamed coconut, roughly
    chopped
450ml boiling water
1 tbsp tomato ketchup
pinch of cayenne pepper
handful of fresh coriander leaves,
    roughly chopped
juice of $\frac{1}{2}$–1 lime
salt and freshly ground black
    pepper
steamed or boiled rice

Heat the oil and sugar in a wide, heavy-based pan, with a lid (or use a deep frying pan and a piece of foil). Caramelise the oil and sugar over a medium heat, taking care not to burn. Add the diced chicken and stir fry until it is golden brown all over. Add the onion, green pepper, garlic and ginger and fry for a further couple of minutes.

Measure the boiling water in a jug, and add the creamed coconut, stirring until it's melted. It doesn't matter if there are a few lumps as they will melt away in the stew. Add to the meat along with the tomato ketchup and cayenne pepper and stir really well. Bring to a gentle simmer, cover with a lid or a tightly-fitting piece of foil and cook over a low heat for about 1 hour, or until the chicken is meltingly tender.

Leave to rest with the lid on for 5 minutes, then skim off any fat that may have separated from the coconut milk. Stir though the chopped coriander and taste the sauce, it will be sweet because of the brown sugar, so add enough lime juice to sharpen it to your liking.

Serve with steamed or boiled rice.

Not suitable for freezing – the peppers will not freeze well and will become mushy on reheating.

Lamb tagine with apricots and almonds

Honey and apricots add plenty of sweetness to this delicately spiced traditional North African tagine. If you like a little heat in your food feel free to add a teaspoon or so of cayenne pepper or a couple of chopped chillies when you marinate the meat.

Serves 4–6 | Takes 15 minutes to make, plus marinating, 2 hours to cook

900g lamb neck fillet, diced in 3cm chunks
4 tbsp olive oil
2 tsp ground cinnamon
2 tsp ground coriander
1 tsp ground ginger
1 tsp ground turmeric
3 green cardamom pods, lightly bruised
4–6 cloves, lightly bruised
1–2 tsp cayenne pepper or dried chilli (optional)
3 cloves garlic, crushed
2 onions, sliced
2 carrots, cut into thick slices
125g dried apricots, halved
100g whole blanched almonds, toasted
400ml vegetable stock or water
2 tsp honey
salt and freshly ground black pepper
buttered couscous, to serve

Place the meat in a large non-metallic bowl, add 2 tablespoons of the olive oil, all of the spices and the garlic, stir well. Cover with clingfilm and leave to marinate in the fridge for a few hours, or longer if you have time.

Once the meat has marinated, add the remaining oil to a large, heavy-based pan with a lid. Fry the onions gently for a few minutes until they soften and begin to colour at the edges. Add the spiced meat, plus all the marinade and cook over a high heat to seal all over.

Stir through the carrots, apricots and almonds and pour over the stock. Lastly add the honey and season with a little salt and freshly ground black pepper. Stir thoroughly and bring up to a gentle simmer. Cover with the lid and cook over a low heat for around 2 hours or until the lamb is very tender and the sauce reduced.

Serve with buttered couscous.

Freeze for up to 3 months. Defrost overnight in the fridge before reheating thoroughly, adding a little water or stock if it is looking dry.

Polish pork and cabbage stew

This allspice-scented stew is loosely based on the Polish national dish of Bigos, also known as hunters stew. I make no claims on authenticity – it doesn't use sauerkraut, which is included in the traditional version, for a start but it is hearty and delicious nonetheless.

Serves 4–6 | Takes 15 minutes to make, plus soaking, $1^{1}/_{4}$–$1^{1}/_{2}$ hours to cook

25g dried porcini mushrooms
10 prunes
500ml boiling water
1 tbsp olive oil
800g pork shoulder, diced into 3cm cubes
140g smoked lardons or pancetta
250g white or green cabbage, shredded
2 carrots, sliced into batons
1 onion, sliced
1 heaped tsp plain flour
2 bay leaves
2 tsp ground allspice
2 tbsp tomato purée
1 tbsp white wine vinegar
2 tsp honey, set or clear
salt and freshly ground black pepper
plain boiled or mashed potatoes, to serve

Soak the dried mushrooms and prunes in the boiling water. Set aside to infuse for 15 minutes or so.

Heat the oil in a large, heavy-based pan or flameproof casserole. Fry the diced pork and lardons in the oil for a few minutes until lightly browned. Add the cabbage, carrots and onion and fry for a further couple of minutes. Add the flour and stir well to coat evenly. Pour in the prunes and mushrooms along with their soaking water, being careful to leave the last little bit of water as it may contain some grit from the mushrooms.

Throw in the bay leaves and allspice and add the tomato purée, white wine vinegar and honey. Season with a little salt and a good grind of black pepper. Bring to the boil, cover and simmer gently for $1^{1}/_{4}$–$1^{1}/_{2}$ hours or until the meat is almost falling apart and the sauce has thickened.

Check the seasoning and adjust as necessary and serve with plain boiled potatoes or creamy mash.

Freeze for up to 3 months. Defrost overnight in the fridge before reheating thoroughly, adding a little water or stock if it is looking dry.

Keralan chicken stew

In Kerala this delicately spiced stew is popular for breakfast. Personally I prefer it for supper but the choice is entirely up to you!

Serves 4–6 | Takes 20 minutes to make, plus marinating, 1–1$\frac{1}{4}$ hours to cook

900g skinless, boneless chicken thighs, cut into 5cm chunks
2 large onions, roughly chopped
50g fresh root ginger, peeled and roughly chopped
5 cloves garlic, roughly chopped
2–4 green chillies, deseeded and roughly chopped
1 tsp ground turmeric
2 tbsp vegetable oil
1 tbsp mustard seeds
1 cinnamon stick
4 cardamom pods, lightly bruised
3 cloves, lightly bruised
$\frac{1}{2}$ tsp black peppercorns, coarsely crushed
400ml can coconut milk
3 medium potatoes, peeled and cut into chunks
200g frozen peas
salt and freshly ground black pepper
basmati rice, to serve

Lay the chicken in a single layer in a non-metallic bowl. In a food processor whizz the onions, ginger, garlic, chillies and turmeric to a thick paste, adding a spoonful or two of cold water to help it blend together. Spread this paste all over the chicken pieces. Cover the chicken with cling film and set the chicken aside in the fridge for 1–2 hours.

In a large, heavy-based pan, with a lid, heat the oil and add the mustard seeds. Fry gently for a minute or so until they start to pop and crackle. Add the marinated chicken, along with the spicy marinade, and fry a little to seal the meat. Then add the remaining spices and pour over the coconut milk. Top up with a little water so the chicken is just covered and bring up to a gentle simmer. Cover with a lid and cook over a low heat for 30 minutes.

Add the potato chunks to the pan, re-cover and continue cooking for a further 30 minutes or until the potatoes are tender but not falling apart. Once the potatoes and chicken are cooked, throw in the peas and allow to cook for a further few minutes.

Taste to check the seasoning, you will probably need to add a little salt. Serve piping hot with plenty of basmati rice to soak up the juices.

Freeze for up to 3 months. Defrost in the fridge overnight before reheating thoroughly in the oven at 160°C/gas 3. Reheating gently in the oven ensures the potatoes don't break up too much, you may need to add a little water or stock if it is looking dry.

Pork braised with ginger, garlic and sweet soy

It is difficult for me to describe just how much I love this dish. I find the sweet saltiness of the soy sauce and the heat from the chilli and ginger almost impossible to resist. It is quite a spicy dish, so use half the quantities of both chillies if you want less heat. I have cooked this so many times for friends and family I could literally do it with my eyes closed. In fact I have even been know to dream about it! So, I really do urge you to give it a go.

Serves 4–6 | Takes 20 minutes to make, 1³/₄ hours to cook

2 tbsp vegetable oil
6 shallots, thinly sliced
6 cloves garlic, crushed
50g fresh root ginger root, peeled and grated
1kg pork shoulder, cut into 3cm chunks
500ml chicken stock
5 tbsp kecap manis (sweet soy sauce)
2 tbsp dark soy sauce
1 tbsp tamarind paste
4 medium hot red chillies, deseeded and chopped
4 red bird's eye chillies, left whole
200g green beans, topped, tailed and halved
salt and freshly ground black pepper

For the garnish
6 shallots finely sliced
5 tbsp vegetable oil
1–2 medium hot red chillies, deseeded and finely sliced

plain steamed or boiled rice, to serve

In a large, heavy-based pan add the oil and fry the shallots over a medium heat until soft and golden. Add the garlic and ginger and cook for a further minute before adding the pork. Allow the pork to cook for a few minutes until it takes on a little colour.

Pour over the stock, followed by both types of soy sauce, the tamarind, the chopped and whole chillies and 1 teaspoon freshly ground black pepper. Bring to the boil, reduce the heat a little and leave to simmer for around 1¹/₂ hours or until the meat is very tender.

Whilst the stew is simmering prepare the garnish, heat the oil in a wok or large frying pan and fry the shallots until they are crisp and golden brown, stir constantly to keep the shallots moving so they don't burn before they have crisped up. Remove with a slotted spoon and drain on kitchen paper. Set aside.

Once the meat is cooked, throw in the green beans, pressing them under the sauce as you go. Cook for a further 5-10 minutes or until the beans are cooked through and the sauce is thick and rich. Check the seasoning you may want to add a little salt.

Transfer to a serving platter and scatter over the crispy fried shallots and the finely sliced red chilli. Serve with plain steamed or boiled rice.

Freeze for up to 3 months. Defrost overnight in the fridge before reheating thoroughly, adding a little water or stock if it is looking dry.

Pork belly braised with satsumas and medieval spices

To me this dish is full of wintry, mulled wine flavours and is perfect for long lazy Sunday lunches with friends. I like to eat this with mashed parsnip or celeriac and dark green cabbage.

Serves 4–6 | Takes 20 minutes to make, plus marinating, $2\frac{1}{2}$–3 hours to cook

1.6kg piece of pork belly
3 fat cloves garlic, cut into strips
1 tsp ground allspice
1 tsp ground ginger
1 tsp ground cinnamon
$\frac{1}{2}$ nutmeg, grated
1 tbsp brown sugar
2 tbsp olive oil
2 large onions, sliced
350ml red wine
2 tbsp red wine vinegar
2 bay leaves
3 cloves
3 satsumas, unpeeled and halved
salt and freshly ground black pepper
mashed parsnip or celeriac and dark green cabbage, to serve

With a sharp knife carefully remove the skin on the pork belly, leaving a 5mm layer of fat. Piece the flesh all over with the knife and poke in the strips of garlic. Combine the allspice, ginger, cinnamon, nutmeg and sugar in a small bowl and stir well, rub the mixture all over the meat. Wrap the pork tightly in clingfilm and leave to marinate in the fridge for a few hours, or overnight if you have time.

When you are ready to cook, preheat the oven to 160°C/gas 3.

In a large, flameproof casserole heat the oil until it is smoking hot. Quickly sear the pork belly on both sides until it gets a lovely golden crust. Remove to a plate and set aside.

Turn down the heat and fry the onions for a few minutes until they are slightly caramelised at the edges. Return the pork belly to the pan, resting it on top of the onions, then pour over the red wine and red wine vinegar. Add enough water to just cover the meat. Tuck in the bay leaves, cloves and satsumas, season with a little salt and black pepper and bring up to a gentle simmer.

Cover with a lid and cook in the oven for a generous $2\frac{1}{2}$ hours by which time the pork will be meltingly tender. Turn the oven off and transfer the pork gently to a plate and put back in the oven to keep warm. Remove the satsumas from the stew and discard they will have imparted their flavour. Thicken the sauce on the hob until it reaches the desired consistency, then taste to check the seasoning.

Carve the pork into thick slices and serve with the sauce drizzled over the top.

Freeze for up to 3 months. Defrost overnight in the fridge before reheating thoroughly in the oven at 160°C/gas 3. Reheating gently in the oven ensures the pork belly heats evenly, you may need to add a little water or stock if it is looking dry.

Beef rendang

Rendang is a rich and aromatic Indonesian stew of beef simmered over a long period of time in a multitude of spices to give a really complex, intense flavour. Traditionally the stew would be cooked for so long that there really is no sauce to speak of, just deeply seasoned pieces of tender meat. I prefer to cook it for a little less time as I like a bit of cooking liquid to soak into the rice I eat with it. I would urge you to use galangal if you can find it – try an Asian supermarket – it looks very similar to ginger root, and comes from the same family, but with its citrus and pine aromas it has quite a different flavour.

Serves 4–6 | Takes 20–25 minutes to make, plus marinating, $2^1/_2$–$3^1/_2$ hours to cook

50g fresh root ginger, peeled and coarsely chopped
30g fresh galangal (or equivalent weight in extra ginger), coarsely chopped
50g garlic cloves
10 shallots, peeled and coarsely chopped
3 lemongrass stalks, coarsely chopped
900g stewing beef (chuck, skirt or braising beef), cut into 3cm cubes
2 tbsp vegetable oil
1 tbsp turmeric powder
1 tbsp ground coriander
2 tsp dried chilli flakes
1 tsp ground cinnamon
4–5 cloves
400ml can coconut milk
2 tbsp desiccated coconut
2 tbsp dark soy sauce
1 tbsp brown sugar
1 tbsp tamarind paste
3–4 kaffir lime leaves
steamed rice, to serve

In a food processor, whizz the ginger, galangal, garlic, shallots and lemongrass to a paste, adding a few tablespoons of cold water if necessary to help it along. Place the beef in a large non-metallic bowl and add the paste, mix well to ensure all the meat is thoroughly coated. Cover with clingfilm and et aside to marinate in the fridge for a few hours – overnight would not hurt.

When you are ready to cook the rendang, heat the oil in a large, heavy-based pan, with a lid, and briefly fry the turmeric, coriander, chilli, cinnamon and cloves. Add the marinated beef and all its juices and fry for a few minutes to seal the meat.

Pour in the coconut milk and add the desiccated coconut, soy sauce and brown sugar. Finally add the tamarind paste and kaffir lime leaves and bring up to a gentle simmer. Cover with a lid, lower the heat to the minimum and cook gently for 1 hour, I find covering with a lid for the initial cooking stage helps the beef to become more tender.

After 1 hour, remove the lid and cook for a further $1^1/_2$ hours, by which time the sauce should be thick and rich. Keep half an eye on it and stir occasionally to stop it from sticking. If you would like a really traditional dry dish, continue cooking for anything up to a further 1 hour until the desired consistency is reached.

Serve with plain steamed rice.

Freeze for up to 3 months. Defrost overnight in the fridge before reheating thoroughly, adding a little water or stock if it is looking dry.

Vietnamese duck and orange

I love the combination of sweet orange with rich duck and this has just enough chilli heat and spice to warm you from the inside out. I like to eat this stew with plain jasmine rice and some stir-fried Oriental greens, such as pak choi.

Serves 4–6 | Takes 15–20 minutes to make, 1$\frac{1}{2}$–2 hours to cook

4–6 duck legs, allow 1 per person
50g fresh root ginger, peeled and finely sliced
5 cloves garlic, finely sliced
juice and zest of 4 large oranges
3 tbsp nam pla (fish sauce)
1 tbsp granulated sugar
4 star anise
4 red bird's eye chillies, deseeded and finely chopped
2 lemongrass stalks, finely sliced
8 spring onions, sliced
1 tbsp cornflour
salt and freshly ground black pepper
2 spring onions, finely shredded, to garnish
jasmine rice and stir-fried Oriental greens, to serve

Prick the duck legs all over with a fork this will help them to release some of their fat. In a heavy-based pan, with a lid, fry the duck on both sides until the skin is crisp and golden. Remove to a plate and set aside.

Pour off all but 2 tablespoons of the fat in the pan and fry the ginger and garlic over a low heat until lightly golden. Return the duck to the pan, along with the orange zest, nam pla, sugar, star anise, chillies, lemongrass and spring onions, stirring well to mix everything thoroughly.

Pour the orange juice into a jug and top up with water to give you 700ml of liquid in total. Pour this over the duck and bring up to a gentle simmer. Cover with a lid and cook gently for 1$\frac{1}{2}$–2 hours or until the duck is falling off the bone.

Carefully remove the duck legs to a warm serving dish, cover tightly with foil and set aside. Mix the cornflour with a little cold water to form a paste and add this to the pan. Bring to the boil and simmer for a few minutes until the sauce is thickened. Taste the sauce to check the seasoning and add a little salt and freshly ground black pepper if necessary.

Pour the sauce over the duck, garnish with the shredded spring onion and serve with the rice and stir-fried greens.

Freeze for up to 3 months. Defrost overnight in the fridge before reheating thoroughly in the oven at 160°C/gas 3. Reheating gently in the oven ensures the duck heats evenly and doesn't break up too much, you may need to add a little water or stock if it is looking dry.

Seafood stew with coconut and Thai holy basil

I love this Thai-inspired stew. The holy basil lends a really aromatic fresh taste to the dish and it is really quick and simple to prepare. Thai holy basil can be found in Asian supermarkets – it tastes quite different from the ubiquitous Italian basil. If you can't get hold of it, substitute coriander leaf. Feel free to vary the type of fish and shellfish you use, just stick loosely to the quantities given and it will be delicious. If you are using crab use a 50:50 mix of brown and white meat; the brown has so much more flavour.

Serves 4–6 | Takes 15 minutes to make, 45 minutes to cook

1 tbsp vegetable oil
6 shallots, finely sliced
50g fresh root ginger, peeled and grated
50g garlic, crushed
400ml can coconut milk
300ml fish stock
2 lemongrass stalks, finely shredded
2–3 kaffir lime leaves (frozen or dried)
2 tbsp Thai red curry paste
3 tbsp nam pla (fish sauce)
100g green beans, topped and tailed
juice of 2 limes
loose handful of Thai holy basil leaves
600g firm white fish fillet, e.g. haddock, cod, pollack, monkfish – cut into portion-sized pieces
250g fresh brown and white crabmeat
10–12 raw tiger prawns, shell on or off
salt and freshly ground black pepper
steamed rice, to serve

Heat the oil in a large, heavy-based pan and gently fry the shallots with the ginger and garlic until they are translucent but not coloured. Pour in the coconut milk and stock, and add the lemongrass, lime leaves, Thai red curry paste and nam pla. Bring up to a gentle simmer and cook, uncovered, for 20–25 minutes.

Add the green beans, lime juice and Thai holy basil leaves, cover and simmer for 5 minutes. Then lay the white fish fillets on top and spoon a little sauce over them. Re-cover and cook for another 5 minutes before gently stirring through the crabmeat and prawns. Simmer until the prawns are pink and cooked all the way through. This will take about 4–6 minutes depending on their size.

Taste to check the seasoning you may want to add a little salt and black pepper. Serve immediately with plenty of steamed rice.

Not suitable for freezing.

African stewed beef with peanut butter

Versions of this stew are found all over the African continent and it's easy to see why. The peanut butter gives the sauce an unusual rich nutty texture. This is great served with plain rice.

Serves 4–6 | Takes 15 minutes to make, 2 hours to cook

2 tbsp vegetable oil
900g braising beef, cut into 3cm
   chunks
2 green peppers, chopped
1 carrot, sliced
1 onion, finely chopped
2 cloves garlic, crushed
400g can chopped tomatoes
300ml beef stock
3 tbsp crunchy peanut butter
1 tsp dried thyme
1 bay leaf
pinch of dried chilli flakes
salt and freshly ground black
   pepper
plain rice, to serve

Heat the oil in a heavy-based pan, with a lid, and quickly brown the beef in two or three batches. Remove to a plate and set aside. Keep the heat high and don't overcrowd the pan or the meat will sweat rather than fry.

Once the meat is browned return it all to the pan, lower the heat a little and add the green peppers, carrot, onion and garlic. Allow the vegetables to soften for a few minutes before pouring in the chopped tomatoes and beef stock and bring up to a steady simmer.

Add the peanut butter, stirring well until it has melted into the sauce, then add the thyme, bay leaf and chilli flakes. Season with a little salt and pepper, go easy on the salt as peanut butter can sometimes be quite salty. You can always add more at the end of cooking.

Reduce the heat to as low as possible, cover with the lid and cook gently for about 2 hours, after which time the meat should be tender and melting.

Check the seasoning and adjust if necessary. Serve with rice.

Freeze for up to 3 months. Defrost overnight in the fridge before reheating thoroughly, adding a little water or stock if it is looking dry.

Caribbean beef stew with lime, ginger and thyme

Marinating the meat before cooking makes all the difference in this flavourful Caribbean stew, so try to leave the beef for as long as you can. If you can't get authentic Caribbean Scotch bonnet chillies feel free to use ordinary red chillies (although you will lose a little of the fragrance the Scotch bonnets bring to the dish). This is great served with plain rice and lime wedges to squeeze over for extra zing.

Serves 4–6 | Takes 15 minutes to make, plus marinating, 2 hours to cook

1 kg braising beef, cut into 3cm chunks
juice and zest of 2 limes
2cm piece fresh root ginger, peeled and grated
3 cloves garlic
1 bunch spring onions, finely sliced
1–2 Scotch bonnet chillies, deseeded
3 sprigs fresh thyme or 1 tsp dried thyme
2 tbsp dark brown sugar
2 tbsp malt vinegar
2 tbsp vegetable oil
500ml beef stock
300g sweet potato, peeled and cut into 3–4cm chunks
salt and freshly ground black pepper
plain rice and lime wedges, to serve

Place the beef in a large non-metallic dish, add the lime juice and zest, ginger, spring onions, chillies, thyme, sugar and vinegar. Leave, covered, in the fridge to infuse for 2–3 hours.

Remove the meat from the marinade, scraping off and reserving as much of the marinade as possible. Heat the oil in a flameproof casserole, add the marinated beef and fry over a high heat until the meat is coloured here and there.

Pour in the stock and the reserved marinade, add the sweet potato and bring everything up to a steady simmer. Cover with a tight-fitting lid, reduce the heat and simmer gently until the beef is really tender. This will take about 2–2½ hours.

Taste to check the seasoning and serve with the rice and lime wedges.

Freeze for up to 3 months. Defrost overnight in the fridge before reheating thoroughly in the oven at 160°C/gas 3. Reheating gently in the oven ensures the sweet potato doesn't break up too much, you may need to add a little water or stock if it is looking dry.

Persian chicken with walnuts and pomegranates

Persian dishes are always subtly spiced and this one is based on a traditional recipe known as Fesenjan. Crushed walnuts are used generously to thicken and enrich the sauce and the exotic pomegranate molasses lend a delicious sweet-sour note.

Serves 4–6 | Takes 15 minutes to make, $1^1/_2$–2 hours to cook

2 tbsp olive oil
800g chicken thighs or legs
2 onions, finely chopped
3 cloves garlic, crushed
1 tsp ground cinnamon
$^1/_2$ tsp ground allspice
500ml chicken stock
2 tbsp pomegranate molasses
200g walnuts, roughly crushed in
   a food processor

To garnish
generous handful of fresh flat-leaf
   parsley, chopped
seeds of 1 pomegranate

couscous or rice and watercress
   salad, to serve

Heat the oil in a heavy-based pan, with a lid, and fry the chicken until golden brown on both sides.

Add the onion, garlic and spices and continue to fry for a further couple of minutes. Pour in the stock, and add the pomegranate molasses and walnuts.

Give everything a really good stir and bring it up to a steady simmer. Cover with the lid and simmer for $1^1/_2$–2 hours or until the chicken is really tender and the sauce has thickened. If the chicken is cooked and the sauce is still a little thin simply remove the chicken to a warm plate, increase the heat and reduce the sauce until it thickens.

Transfer the stew to a serving dish and scatter over the parsley and pomegranate seeds. Serve with couscous or rice and a simple watercress salad.

Freeze the stew, ungarnished, for up to 3 months. Defrost overnight in the fridge before reheating thoroughly in the oven at 160°C/ gas 3. Reheating gently in the oven ensures the chicken heats evenly, you may need to add a little water or stock if it is looking dry. After heating garnish with the parsley and pomegranate seeds.

Spiced braised shallots, chickpeas and prunes with herbed couscous

The prunes add an amazing velvety texture to this subtly spiced stew. I like to use banana shallots also known as eschallions, because they can be cut into long strips. But ordinary, round shallots would work perfectly well too.

Serves 4–6 | Takes 15–20 minutes to make, 1–1$\frac{1}{4}$ hours to cook

**250g dried chickpeas, soaked
    overnight in plenty of cold
    water, drained and rinsed
2 tbsp olive oil
25g unsalted butter
12 banana shallots or 20 round
    shallots, cut lengthways into
    slices
1 tbsp cumin seeds
1 tsp ground cinnamon
1 tsp ground coriander
1 tsp ground cumin
3 cloves garlic, sliced
1 litre vegetable stock
200g pitted prunes, halved
salt and freshly ground black
    pepper**

**For the herbed couscous
500g couscous
approximately 600ml boiling
    vegetable stock
25g butter, cut into small dice
small bunch of fresh flat-leaf
    parsley, roughly chopped
small bunch of fresh coriander,
    roughly chopped
small bunch of fresh chives,
    snipped**

Heat the olive oil and butter in a large, heavy-based pan and gently fry the shallots with the cumin seeds until they are very soft. This will take a good 10 minutes or so. Once they are soft turn up the heat a little and allow to caramelise lightly at the edges. Add the ground spices and garlic and stir well to mix.

Add the chickpeas to the pan, along with the vegetable stock. Bring it the boil and cook rapidly for 10 minutes. Reduce the heat to a steady simmer, cover the pan and cook for 45 minutes. Add the prunes and simmer for a further 30 minutes or so until the chickpeas are tender.

About 10 minutes before the stew is ready make the herbed couscous. Place the couscous in a large bowl and pour over enough boiling stock so that they are covered by just over 5mm of liquid. Stir through the butter, herbs and a generous seasoning of salt and black pepper. Cover tightly with clingfilm and allow to rest in a warm place for 10 minutes before forking through the grains to separate them.

Season the stew to taste with salt and freshly ground black pepper and served spooned over the couscous.

Freeze the stew for up to 3 months. Defrost overnight in the fridge before reheating thoroughly, adding a little water or stock if it is looking dry. Couscous not suitable for freezing.

Chile verde

Chile verde or Mexican green chilli stew is ubiquitous across Mexico where every household will have their own tried and tested recipe, sometimes using pork instead of beef. Here is my version. If I can get hold of them, I use unripe green tomatoes to enhance the 'greenness' of the finished dish. The number of chillies may seem very high, but these green chillies are generally very mild. So if you like things spicy use the full quantity, or simply go for fewer if you want less heat.

Serves 4–6 | Takes 40 minutes to make, 2$\frac{1}{2}$ hours to cook

10–20 long, green chillies
2 tbsp vegetable oil
900g beef shin, cut into 2cm cubes
2 onions, chopped
3 cloves garlic, crushed
4 medium green or red tomatoes, roughly chopped
3 medium potatoes, peeled and cut into 3cm chunks
2 tbsp ground cumin
600ml beef stock
salt and freshly ground black pepper
rice or flour tortillas, to serve

Preheat the oven to 200°C/gas 6.

Lay the chillies on a baking tray and roast in the oven for 20–30 minutes, or until they are soft and the skin is starting to blacken and blister. Transfer to a bowl and cover with clingfilm until cool enough to handle. Peel the chillies, either removing the seeds or leaving them in if you prefer extra heat. Don't worry about bits of peel here and there, just get rid of as much as you can. Chop coarsely and set aside.

Whilst the chillies are roasting, heat the oil in a large, heavy-based pan, with a lid, and brown the beef quickly on all sides. Do this in two or three batches if necessary to avoid overcrowding the pan. Transfer the beef to plate and lower the heat.

Fry the onion for around 5 minutes or until it is soft and starting to colour a little at the edges. Add the garlic and fry for a further minute or so before returning all the beef to the pan.

Add the tomatoes, potatoes, cumin and beef stock, and the peeled and chopped green chillies. Season with salt and black pepper and bring up to a gentle simmer. Cover with a lid and simmer for 2 hours. Uncover and cook for a further 30 minutes to allow the sauce to thicken.

Taste to check the seasoning and serve with plenty of rice or flour tortillas.

Freeze for up to 3 months. Defrost overnight in the fridge before reheating thoroughly, adding a little water or stock if it is looking dry.

Cardamom and black pepper chicken

I love this fragrant Indian curry which takes its heat from spicy black peppercorns rather than chillies.

Serves 4–6 | Takes 20 minutes to make, plus marinating, 1½ hours to cook

For the marinade
2 onions, roughly chopped
50g fresh root ginger, peeled and roughly chopped
5 cloves garlic, roughly chopped
2 tsp black peppercorns, roughly ground
1 tsp cayenne pepper
½ tsp salt
800g skinless, boneless chicken thighs, cut into 5cm chunks

For the stew
8 green cardamom pods
2 tsp cumin seeds
1 tsp coriander seeds
1 tsp ground cinnamon
1 tbsp vegetable oil
600ml boiling water
200g green beans, topped and tailed
4 tbsp full-fat natural yogurt
steamed rice, to serve

Begin by marinating the chicken. In a food processor blend together the onion, ginger and garlic with 4–5 tablespoons cold water to form a thick paste. Add the ground pepper, cayenne pepper and salt. Place the chicken in a non-metallic bowl and rub the marinade all over. Cover with clingfilm and leave in the fridge for 3–4 hours.

Once the chicken has finished marinating, start the stew by roughly grinding together the cardamom pods, cumin seeds, coriander seeds and cinnamon. Heat the oil in a heavy-based pan, with a lid, and fry the spices very briefly, no more than 20–30 seconds, before adding the meat and all its marinade. Stir-fry the meat in the spices for a few minutes and then add the boiling water. Bring up to a simmer, cover with the lid and cook gently for 1¼ hours by which time the chicken should be very tender and the sauce reduced.

Add the green beans to the stew, re-cover and cook for a further 10–15 minutes or until the beans are tender. If the sauce is a little thin at this stage leave the lid off whilst the beans are cooking but try to keep them submerged so they cook evenly.

Once the beans are tender, turn off the heat, stir through the yogurt and serve immediately with plenty of steamed rice.

If you want to freeze this dish do not add the yogurt. Freeze for up to 3 months. Defrost overnight in the fridge before reheating thoroughly. Once it is hot, add the yogurt as in the recipe above.

Lamb cooked in garam masala

Despite the rather long ingredients list this is really very simple to make. Once you have made the garam masala spice blend, it's simply a question of adding it to the lamb and vegetables and leaving it to cook long and slow. You can also make this with lamb shanks if you prefer but they would take an extra 30 minutes or so to cook.

Serves 4–6 | Takes 20 minutes to make, 2–2$^1/_2$ hours to cook

For the garam masala
2 tbsp fennel seeds, roughly ground
1 tbsp paprika
1 tsp ground mace
1 tsp ground nutmeg
1 tsp ground cinnamon
1 tsp ground ginger
1 tsp cayenne pepper
3 bay leaves, finely chopped
$^1/_2$ tsp salt

For the stew
1 tbsp vegetable oil
900g lamb neck fillet, diced into 3cm cubes
3 onions, chopped
2 green peppers, chopped
12 cherry tomatoes, halved
60g fresh root ginger, peeled and grated
4 cloves garlic, chopped
2–4 medium hot green chillies, deseeded and chopped
salt and freshly ground black pepper

handful of fresh coriander leaves, roughly chopped, to garnish
lemon wedges, to serve

Make the garam masala by simply mixing all the ingredients in a small bowl. Set aside.

In a large heavy-based pan, with a lid, heat the oil and lightly brown the lamb on all sides. Add the onions, green pepper and cherry tomatoes and continue to fry for a few minutes until they starts to soften a little at the edges. Stir in the garam masala spice blend and fry briefly for 20–30 seconds, being careful that the spices do not burn or they will become bitter.

Add the ginger, garlic and green chillies and pour over 750ml water. Bring up to a gentle simmer, cover with a lid and cook slowly for at least 2 hours or until the lamb is really soft and melting. It may take a little longer. Remove the lid about halfway through cooking to allow the sauce to gently thicken.

Check the seasoning you may need to add a little more salt. Garnish with the coriander leaves and serve with the lemon wedges.

Not suitable for freezing.

Chicken tagine with harissa and chickpeas

Moroccan tagines are generally mild and sweetly spiced but this chicken version is spiced up at the end of cooking with the fiery but fragrant harissa paste. Harissa paste varies hugely from make to make – taste a little first to gauge the heat it gives. If you like the hot stuff add more, if not add a little less. Serve with buttered, steamed couscous.

Serves 4–6 | Takes 10–15 minutes to make, 1–1$\frac{1}{2}$ hours to cook

2 tbsp olive oil
1kg chicken thighs, or a combination of thighs and drumsticks
2 carrots, roughly chopped
2 onions, roughly chopped
2 cloves garlic, crushed
1 tsp ground cinnamon
1 tsp ground ginger
2 x 400g cans chickpeas, drained and rinsed
600ml chicken stock
1–2 tbsp harissa paste
salt and freshly ground black pepper
generous handful of fresh coriander leaves, chopped, to garnish
buttered, steamed couscous, to serve

Heat the oil in a large, flameproof casserole and fry the chicken legs on both sides until they are a good golden colour. Toss in the carrots, onions and garlic along with the cinnamon and ginger and fry for a further couple of minutes, stirring well to coat the meat with the spices.

Add the stock and chickpeas and stir thoroughly, bring to a steady simmer. Turn down the heat, cover with a lid and cook gently for around 1–1$\frac{1}{2}$ hours or until the chicken is virtually falling off the bone.

When the chicken is cooked, gently stir through the harissa paste and check the seasoning. You may want to add a little black pepper and it will almost certainly need some salt. If the sauce is a little thin carefully lift out the chicken to a plate and keep warm by covering tightly in foil, turn up the heat and reduce to the desired consistency.

Serve the tagine spooned over the top of buttered couscous and finish with a generous scattering of chopped coriander leaves.

Freeze the stew, ungarnished, for up to 3 months. Defrost overnight in the fridge before reheating thoroughly in the oven at 160°C/ gas 3. Reheating gently in the oven ensures the chicken heats evenly, you may need to add a little water or stock if it is looking dry.

Lamb with dried figs and star anise

Figs and star anise go brilliantly together, the aniseed flavour of the spice cutting through the sweetness of the dried fruit. The vaguely Oriental flavours of this stew make steamed basmati rice and wilted pak choi the perfect partners.

Serves 4–6 | Takes 10–15 minutes to make, 2 hours to cook

1 tbsp plain flour
900g lamb neck fillet, cut in 3cm cubes
2–3 tbsp vegetable oil
8 shallots, peeled and cut in half
3 cloves garlic, sliced
200g dried figs, halved
3 star anise
2 wide strips of lemon peel
400ml lamb or vegetable stock
200ml red wine
salt and freshly ground black pepper
steamed basmati rice and wilted pak choi, to serve

Season the flour with salt and freshly ground black pepper. Toss the lamb cubes in the seasoned flour.

Heat 2 tablespoons of the oil in a large, heavy-based pan, with a lid, until it is smoking hot. Quickly sear the lamb on all sides until nicely browned. Do this in two or three batches if necessary, transferring to a plate as each piece is browned.

Reduce the heat, add a splash more oil if necessary and fry the shallots for a few minutes until they are a little coloured here and there. Add the garlic, figs, star anise and lemon peel and cook for a further minute or so.

Pour over the stock and wine and bring up to a gentle simmer. Cover with the lid and cook over a low heat for about 2 hours, or until the lamb falls apart when gently teased with a fork. Remove the lid halfway through cooking to allow the sauce to thicken gently.

Taste to check the seasoning and serve with plenty of basmati rice and wilted pak choi.

Freeze the stew for up to 3 months. Defrost overnight in the fridge before reheating thoroughly, adding a little water or stock if it is looking dry.

FRESH AND VIBRANT

Although autumn and winter are the more obvious seasons for hearty stews there are plenty of lighter, brighter ways to stew food too. Heady with the scent of fresh herbs and a great way of using a glut of cheap seasonal vegetables these recipes prove you don't need to be constrained by cool weather to make a delicious stew. And as another bonus, these recipes tend to be quicker and slicker to make – just what you need as the weather warms up and you don't want to stay in the kitchen for long.

Chicken with courgettes, lemon and marjoram

Courgette plants are voracious things, and this dish was designed to use the glut of fruit borne from my two plants last summer. Fresh marjoram is not widely available from the supermarket but it is ridiculously easy to grow – one small plant will soon become a lush clump provided it gets plenty of sunshine. But substitute fresh thyme or oregano if you need to.

Serves 4–6 | Takes 20 minutes to make, plus marinating, $1^1/_2$ hours to cook

For the marinade
1kg chicken legs
300ml white wine
100ml extra virgin olive oil
4 cloves garlic, sliced
generous bunch of marjoram or oregano, woody stems discarded and leaves picked
salt and freshly ground black pepper

For the stew
2–3 tbsp olive oil
3 courgettes, cut into 2cm slices
200ml chicken stock
1 lemon, sliced

buttery new potatoes, to serve

Place the chicken legs in a single layer in a non-metallic dish. Add the wine, garlic, marjoram and a generous seasoning of salt and pepper and turn the legs to coat in the marinade. Cover with clingfilm and leave to infuse for a few hours in the fridge, or overnight if you have time.

When you are ready to begin cooking preheat the oven to 180°C/gas 4.

Heat 2 tablespoons of the oil in a large flameproof casserole until smoking hot. Fry the courgette slices, a few at a time, until they get a little colour on both sides. You are looking for dark patches of caramelisation here and there. Transfer to a plate and set aside.

Lift the chicken out of the dish, scraping off as much juice as you can, reserve the marinade. Add a splash more oil to the casserole if necessary and fry the chicken on both sides until golden brown and crisp. Pour over the reserved marinade and the chicken stock and tuck in the lemon slices. Bring up to a gentle simmer, cover and cook in the oven for around an hour and twenty minutes or until the chicken is tender.

Add the fried courgettes to the casserole, pushing them under the sauce. Return to the oven and cook, uncovered, for a further 5–10 minutes, or until they are tender.

Taste to check the seasoning and serve with buttery new potatoes.

Not suitable for freezing.

Portuguese pork with red peppers

This stewed pork feels summery because it's sharp with the scent of lemons and full of sweet red peppers. It is delicious served with simple buttery new potatoes and perhaps some salad leaves to mop in the moreish sauce.

Serves 4–6 | Takes 15–20 minutes to make, plus marinating, 1$\frac{1}{2}$ hours to cook

900g pork shoulder, cut into 3cm cubes
200ml white wine
zest and juice 2 lemons
3 tbsp olive oil
4 cloves garlic, crushed
pinch of dried red chilli flakes
2 tbsp olive oil
6 shallots, peeled and halved
3 large red peppers, deseeded and sliced into strips
500ml chicken stock
salt and freshly ground black pepper
generous handful of fresh flat-leaf parsley, roughly chopped, to garnish
buttery new potatoes and salad leaves, to serve

Place the pork in a shallow, non-metallic dish and add the white wine, lemon zest and juice, olive oil and garlic. Season well, cover with clingfilm and leave to marinate in the fridge for 2–3 hours.

When you are ready to begin making the stew, remove the pork from the marinade, scraping off and reserving as much of the sauce as possible. Heat half the oil in a large, heavy-based pan and fry the pork quickly on all sides until it is seared golden brown. Do this in two or three batches to give the meat space to colour. Once the last batch is done set the meat to one side.

Add the remaining oil to the pan and fry the shallots and peppers over a hot heat until they start to caramelise a little at the edges. Return the meat to the pan along with the reserved marinade. Add the stock, bring to the boil, cover and simmer for about 1$\frac{1}{2}$ hours or until the pork is meltingly soft.

Garnish with the parsley and serve with the potatoes and salad leaves.

Not suitable for freezing.

Chakchouka

This Tunisian spiced vegetable dish with egg is a really unusual and subtly spiced stew. In North Africa cooking eggs like this is common and I love the way they poach gently on top of the stew.

Serves 4–6 | Takes 15 minutes to make, 25–30 minutes to cook

2 tsp cumin seeds
1 tsp caraway seeds
2 tbsp olive oil
3 red peppers, sliced
3 green peppers, sliced
3 cloves garlic, sliced
2 x 400g cans chopped tomatoes
4–6 large eggs, 1 per person
salt and freshly ground black
   pepper
handful of fresh coriander leaves,
   roughly chopped, to garnish
extra virgin olive oil and bread, to
   serve

In a large, deep frying pan, with a lid, dry-fry the cumin and caraway seeds for a couple of minutes, taking care not to burn the spices or they will go bitter. As soon as you begin to smell their aroma wafting up from the pan tip them into a pestle and mortar and roughly crush.

To the same pan, add the olive oil and fry the peppers over a medium high heat for 10 minutes, or until they just start to catch a little at the edges. Add the garlic and crushed spices and fry for another minute, then pour in the tomatoes and bring up to a simmering point. Season with a little salt and pepper, turn the heat down and cook with the lid on for 15–20 minutes or until the peppers are soft and surrounded by a thick tomato sauce.

Using the back of a wooden spoon, make little hollows in the surface of the stew, break in the eggs, seasoning the top of each with some salt and pepper. Cover with the lid and allow the eggs to gently cook for 4–7 minutes depending on how you like them cooked.

Remove from the heat and serve scattered with the coriander and a little extra virgin olive oil. Plenty of bread is essential to mop up all the delicious juices.

Not suitable for freezing

Chicken stew with leeks and Chantenay carrots

The gems in this stew are the whole Chantenay carrots that nestle amongst the chicken offering mini bursts of sweetness. These carrots, incidentally, are the only ones I've ever had any success growing at home and they are really popular with my kids.

Serves 4–6 | Takes 15 minutes to make, 1$\frac{1}{2}$ hours to cook

2 tbsp plain flour
1kg chicken thighs, bone in
1 tbsp olive oil
2 large leeks, washed thoroughly and sliced into chunks
250g Chantenay carrots, whole and unpeeled
2 tbsp fresh thyme leaves
2 cloves garlic, crushed
500ml chicken stock
150ml white wine
salt and freshly ground black pepper
new potatoes with butter and fresh herbs, to serve

Season the flour with salt and freshly ground black pepper.

On a large plate roll the chicken pieces in the seasoned flour, making sure they are well coated all over.

Heat the olive oil in a large, flameproof casserole or large, heavy-based pan with a lid. Fry the chicken pieces a few at a time until they are golden brown all over, transferring to a plate whilst you cook the remaining pieces. Set the chicken aside.

Reduce the heat and add the leeks and carrots to the casserole. Fry for a couple of minutes, being careful not to let the leeks burn. Return the chicken to the casserole, along with the thyme and garlic and give everything a good stir.

Pour over the stock and wine, bring up to the boil then cover with the lid. Reduce the heat and simmer gently for around 1$\frac{1}{2}$ hours, or until the chicken is just starting to fall off the bone. If the sauce is a little thin remove the lid for the final 30 minutes of cooking to allow it to thicken slightly.

Serve with new potatoes crushed lightly with lots of butter and fresh herbs.

Freeze for up to 3 months. Defrost overnight in the fridge before reheating thoroughly, adding a little water if it seems a little dry.

Sea bream with asparagus, new potatoes and Noilly Prat

This recipe is designed to make the most of the wonderful, if brief, British asparagus season. If bream is hard to find any firm-fleshed white fish fillets will work just fine. Crusty bread with lots of butter is just the thing to soak up the fragrant juices.

Serves 4–6 | Takes 15–20 minutes to make, 35–40 minutes to cook

70g unsalted butter
2 onions, finely sliced
3 cloves garlic, crushed
500g new potatoes, thickly sliced
200ml Noilly Prat or other white vermouth
600ml vegetable stock
2 tbsp fresh tarragon leaves, roughly chopped
2 bunches asparagus, cut into 4cm pieces
4–6 bream fillets
salt and freshly ground black pepper
crusty bread and butter, to serve

Melt 50g of the butter in a heavy-based pan, with a lid, and gently sweat the onions until they are meltingly soft. This will take about 10 minutes don't rush it, you are not looking to colour the onions at all.

Add the garlic and sliced potatoes and stir well to coat in the buttery juices. Pour in the Noilly Prat, turn the heat up slightly and allow to reduce for a few minutes before adding the vegetable stock and tarragon. Season with a little salt and freshly ground black pepper and bring up to a simmer. Reduce the heat, cover and cook for about 20–25 minutes or until the potatoes are just tender.

Add the asparagus and stir well to submerge the stems in the stew. Gently lay the fish fillets on top of the stew, dotting each with a little of the remaining butter and a grind of salt and pepper. Re-cover the pan and simmer for a further 10–15 minutes after which the asparagus should be tender and the fish cooked through.

Check and adjust the seasoning and serve immediately with crusty bread and butter.

Not suitable for freezing.

FISH

Sri Lankan salmon curry with coconut sambal

In this classic Sri Lankan curry, tamarind adds a characteristically sour note that works brilliantly with the sweet tomatoes and coconut milk. The curry itself is mild and aromatic, but the coconut sambal served alongside can be made as fiery as you dare...!

Serves 4–6 | Takes 15 minutes to make, 40–45 minutes to cook

2 tbsp coriander seeds
1 tbsp cumin seeds
1 tsp fenugreek seeds
1 tsp ground turmeric
1/2 tsp ground cinnamon
8 black peppercorns
3 cloves
2 tbsp vegetable oil
2 onions, finely sliced
3 cloves garlic, crushed
100g creamed coconut, roughly chopped
400ml boiling water
400g can chopped tomatoes
1 tbsp tamarind paste
750g salmon fillet, cut into 3cm wide strips
salt

For the coconut sambal
1 tsp Thai shrimp paste
flesh of 1/2 fresh coconut, finely grated or 4 tbsp frozen grated coconut
1 red onion, finely grated
2–4 green chillies, deseeded and finely chopped
juice of 1 lime
1 tomato, grated
1–2 tbsp chopped fresh mint leaves
1 tsp caster sugar

steamed rice, to serve

In a frying pan dry-fry the coriander, cumin and fenugreek seeds for 1–2 minutes. As soon as you smell their fragrance lifting from the pan tip them into a pestle and mortar. Add the cinnamon, turmeric, peppercorns and cloves and grind coarsely.

Heat the oil in a large, heavy-based pan, with a lid, and fry the onions with the spice powder until they start to soften and colour a little. Add the garlic and fry for a further minute.

Add the creamed coconut to the pan, along with the boiling water and tomatoes, stirring thoroughly until the coconut has dissolved. Stir through the tamarind paste and a little salt and bring up to a steady simmer. Allow to cook, uncovered for 20–25 minutes.

Whilst the stew is simmering, prepare the sambal. Spoon the shrimp paste into the centre of a piece of foil and wrap into a little parcel. In a frying pan dry-fry the parcel for 1 minute on each side, then remove from the heat and allow to cool. Mix the cooked shrimp paste with the coconut, red onion, chillies and lime juice. Add the grated tomato, mint, sugar and a little salt to taste, stir thoroughly and set aside to let the flavours to mingle.

Carefully place the fish fillet strips into the sauce and press them gently under the liquid. Cover with the lid and allow to cook for 8–10 minutes or until the fish flakes easily.

Serve spooned over steamed rice with the fiery sambal on the side.

Not suitable for freezing.

Broad bean, pea and Parmesan braise

It has taken me a long, long time to like broad beans – childhood memories of tough leathery beans smothered in thick cheese sauce put me off for years. Then I had a revelation – to enjoy them at their best they really do need to be double-skinned, so each bean is squeezed out of its tough outer skin. A lot of my friends think this is a bit of a faff, but for me it makes them not only palatable but completely delicious. I'll leave you to make your own mind up. I like to eat this with toasted ciabatta drizzled with plenty of extra virgin olive oil.

Serves 4–6 | Takes 10–15 minutes to make, 20 minutes to cook

1 tbsp olive oil
50g unsalted butter
2 onions, finely sliced
500g fresh or frozen broad beans
2 cloves garlic, crushed
300ml vegetable stock
200ml white wine
500g fresh or frozen peas
handful of fresh flat-leaf parsley, roughly chopped
handful of fresh basil, roughly chopped
100g Parmesan cheese, finely grated
salt and freshly ground black pepper
toasted ciabatta and extra virgin olive oil, to serve

Heat the oil and butter in a wide, heavy-based pan and fry the onions gently until they are completely soft and melting, but not coloured. This will take around 10 minutes, so be patient.

Whilst the onions are cooking, blanch the broad beans for 3 minutes in boiling water. Drain, and allow to cool for a few minutes before squeezing them out of their shells. Feel free to skip this step if you like the beans with their skins on.

Add the garlic to the onions in the pan and fry for 1 minute or so. Pour in the stock and the wine and bring up to a steady simmer. Allow to bubble away, uncovered, for 10 minutes to allow the sauce to reduce and concentrate. Then add the broad beans and peas and season generously with salt and black pepper. Simmer for a further 10 minutes or until the vegetables are tender.

Remove from the heat, stir through the herbs and sprinkle the Parmesan over. Serve with the toasted ciabatta drizzled with extra virgin olive oil.

Freeze for up to 3 months. Defrost overnight in the fridge before reheating thoroughly, adding a little water or stock if it seems a little dry.

Chicken with tarragon and sherry vinegar

This is my version of the French classic *Poulet au vinaigre*. It is quite delicious and, despite the crème fraîche, manages to be quite light. I love to eat this with rice, either brown or wild, and a simple green salad.

Serves 4–6 |Takes 15–20 minutes to make, 1–1$^{1}/_{4}$ hours to cook

900g chicken thighs, bone in and skin on
2 tbsp olive oil
10 shallots, peeled and left whole
4 cloves garlic, peeled and bruised
400ml chicken stock
200ml sherry vinegar
1 bunch of fresh tarragon, leaves roughly chopped
3 tbsp crème fraîche
salt and freshly ground black pepper
brown or wild rice and a green salad, to serve

Generously season the chicken thighs on both sides with salt and black pepper.

Heat the oil in a wide pan into which the chicken will fit in a single layer a deep frying pan is ideal. Fry the chicken, a few pieces at a time, until crisp and golden, transferring each piece to a plate as it is done. Set aside.

Add the shallots to the pan and fry for a few minutes until they are coloured a little here and there. Then add the cloves of garlic and cook for 1 minute. Return the chicken to the pan, along with any accumulated juices. Pour in the stock and vinegar and add half the tarragon. Bring up to the boil, then reduce the heat to as low as possible and cook, uncovered, for a generous hour or so until the chicken is tender.

Carefully transfer the chicken to a serving dish and keep warm. Turn up the heat and boil the sauce rapidly for a few minutes until it is thick and glossy. Remove from the heat and stir through the crème fraîche, tasting to check the seasoning.

Garnish with the remaining tarragon and serve with the sauce, rice and a green salad.

Freeze for up to 3 months. Defrost overnight in the fridge before reheating thoroughly, adding a little water if it seems a little dry.

Summer lamb with sun-dried tomatoes, capers and basil

Generous handfuls of freshly torn basil are added to this delicious tomato-based stew just before serving to give it a real burst of summer flavour. It is lovely served with nutty wild rice.

Serves 4–6 | Takes minutes 15 minutes to make, 2 hours to cook

2 tbsp olive oil
900g lamb neck fillet, cut into 3cm cubes
12 shallots, peeled and left whole
4 cloves garlic, crushed
175ml white wine
500ml lamb or vegetable stock
3 tbsp sun-dried tomato purée
3 tbsp capers, salted or in brine, rinsed and drained
3 small bunches basil, leaves roughly torn
salt and freshly ground black pepper
extra virgin olive oil, to drizzle
wild rice, to serve

In a large, heavy-based pan, with a lid, heat the oil until it is smoking and brown the pieces of lamb quickly on all sides. Add the shallots and continue to fry over a medium-high heat until they start to caramelise a little on the edges. Add the garlic and fry for 1 minute, stirring all the time to ensure it doesn't burn.

Pour in the wine and let it bubble and reduce, carefully scraping the base of the pan to release all the delicious sticky caramelised bits that will add loads of flavour to the stew. Once the wine has reduced add the stock and sun-dried tomato paste and bring up to a gentle simmer. Lower the heat, season with a little salt and pepper, cover and simmer slowly for around $1\frac{1}{2}$ hours. Stir from time to time to make sure it's not catching on the base of the pan.

Stir through the capers and cook for a further 30 minutes, with the lid off, to allow the sauce to thicken gently.

Once the lamb is meltingly tender, remove from the heat and stir through the basil leaves. Taste to check the seasoning and adjust if necessary. Serve with a little drizzle of extra virgin olive oil over the top and the rice.

Freeze for up to 3 months. Defrost overnight in the fridge before reheating thoroughly, adding a little water if it seems a little dry.

Fish tagine with chermoula

Chermoula is a fragrant spice and herb paste used in Moroccan and Tunisian cooking, usually in fish and seafood dishes. This dish has plenty of potatoes and other vegetables in it so it really doesn't need any accompaniment, although a little bread to soak up the spiced juices would be delicious.

Serves 4–6 | Takes 20 minutes to make, plus marinating, 30 minutes to cook

For the chermoula
2 tsp cumin seeds
small bunch of fresh coriander, roughly chopped
3 garlic cloves, roughly chopped
1 red chilli, deseeded and chopped
pinch of saffron threads
4tbsp extra virgin olive oil
juice of 1 lemon
2 tsp paprika
1 tsp salt

For the tagine
4–6 firm white fish fillets, eg monkfish, sea bass, cod or haddock, cut into serving-sized portions
3 tbsp olive oil
2 onions, sliced
2 red peppers, deseeded and sliced
400g waxy new potatoes, quartered
150g cherry tomatoes, halved
100g green beans, cut in halved
generous handful of black olives
freshly ground black pepper

crusty bread, to serve

Begin by making the chermoula paste. In a small, heavy frying pan toast the cumin seeds for 1 minute or so. Take care not to burn them as soon as you smell their aroma rising from the pan tip into a pestle and mortar and grind to a coarse powder. Put the ground cumin into a blender and process with all the other chermoula ingredients.

Place the fish fillets in a single layer in a shallow dish. Spread half the chermoula paste over the fish fillets, rub it in well, cover with clingfilm and refrigerate for an hour or so.

When the fish is ready to be cooked, heat the oil in a heavy-based pan, with a tight-fitting lid, or a tagine dish if you have one. Fry the onions and peppers over a medium high heat until they start to soften and colour a little at the edges. Add the potatoes and tomatoes and enough water to barely cover everything. Bring up to a simmer and cook for around 15 minutes, or until the potatoes are starting to soften.

Stir through the green beans, olives and the remaining chermoula paste. Season with a generous grinding of black pepper. Gently lay the marinated fish fillets on top of the vegetables and re-cover with the lid. Cook gently for 10–15 minutes or until the fish is cooked through and the vegetables are tender. Serve whilst steaming hot with crusty bread.

Not suitable for freezing.

Lamb with white beans and coriander

This dish is a loose interpretation of an Algerian stew where white beans are cooked for a very long time with a little mutton and plenty of onions and tomatoes. I have changed the quantities to give a more even balance of meat and pulses and added lemon to give it a fresh zesty taste. It is delicious served with a salad of lush ripe tomatoes drizzled with plenty of really good quality olive oil.

Serves 4–6 | Takes 15 minutes to make, 1^3/$_4$ hours to cook

**500g dried haricot beans, soaked
overnight in plenty of cold
water, drained and rinsed**
**500g lamb neck fillet, diced into
3cm cubes**
2–3 tbsp olive oil
3 onions, sliced
3 cloves garlic, crushed
1 tbsp harissa paste
**1–1.5 litres lamb or vegetable
stock**
juice of 1 lemon
**large bunch of fresh coriander,
roughly chopped**
**salt and freshly ground black
pepper**
extra virgin olive oil, to drizzle
tomato salad, to serve

In a large, heavy-based pan heat 2 tablespoons of the oil until it is smoking hot. Quickly fry the lamb on all sides until brown, in batches, transferring each piece to a plate as it is done. Set aside.

Reduce the heat a little and add a splash more oil to the pan if necessary. Fry the onions for 5 minutes or so until they are softening and caramelising a little at the edges. Then add the garlic and fry for 1 minute. Add the drained and rinsed beans, stir through the harissa paste and pour in enough of the stock to cover everything by a generous few centimetres. Reserve the rest of the stock as you may need to add a little more during cooking. Turn the heat up, bring up to the boil and cook for

10 minutes. This step is important to ensure the beans get thoroughly cooked.

Reduce the heat to a steady simmer and return the meat and any accumulated juices to the pan. Cover with a lid and simmer for around 1^1/$_2$ hours or until the lamb is very tender and the beans are soft but not disintegrating. Towards the end of cooking keep checking the levels of liquid – the beans need to stay just submerged – so add a little more stock now and then if necessary.

Stir through the lemon juice and coriander and season generously to taste with salt and freshly ground black pepper. Serve drizzled with extra virgin olive oil and a tomato salad.

Freeze for up to 3 months. Defrost overnight in the fridge before reheating thoroughly, adding a little water if it seems a little dry.

Lamb, petit pois and little gem lettuce with mint

The inspiration for this dish is the French bistro classic *Petit pois à la Française*, one of my very favourite spring dishes where lettuce leaves are gently braised with peas and enriched with a little butter. In this dish the lamb is stewed slowly until tender before the peas and lettuce are added at the final moment.

Serves 4–6 | Takes 15 minutes to make, 2 hours to cook

**2 tbsp olive oil
800g lamb neck fillet, cut into 3cm cubes
2 onions, sliced
4 cloves garlic, sliced
500ml vegetable stock
200g fresh or frozen petit pois
3 little gem lettuce, washed and leaves separated
generous bunch of fresh mint, leaves torn
50g unsalted butter
salt and freshly ground black pepper
new potatoes, to serve**

Preheat the oven to 160˚C/gas 3.

Heat the olive oil in a large, flameproof casserole and fry the cubes of lamb in the very hot oil briefly until they are golden-brown. Add the onions and fry for a few minutes until they start to soften, then add the garlic and cook for 1 minute.

Pour in the stock and bring up to simmering point. Cover with a tight-fitting lid and cook in the oven for $1^1/_2$–$1^3/_4$ hours or until the lamb is very tender and succulent.

Remove from the oven, carefully add the peas, lettuce, mint and butter. Re-cover and return to the oven for 15 minutes by which time the peas will be soft and the lettuce will have wilted.

Taste to check the seasoning and serve with new potatoes.

Not suitable for freezing.

Prawns and red peppers with almond and garlic sauce

A Catalan almond and garlic sauce, called *picada*, makes this dish really special. It is quite pungent and stirred through the stew at the last minute to thicken it slightly and add a real flavour boost. I like to eat this with crisp potato wedges and a green salad.

Serves 4–6 | Takes 10 minutes to make, 20 minutes to cook

2 tbsp olive oil
2 red onions, sliced
2 red peppers, deseeded and sliced
2 cloves garlic
1 tsp Spanish smoked paprika
800g ripe tomatoes, skinned and
    chopped
300ml white wine
500–600g shelled raw king prawns
salt and freshly ground black
    pepper

For the almond and garlic sauce
50g blanched almonds
4 tbsp olive oil
2 slices white bread, crusts
    removed
3 cloves garlic, crushed
loose handful of fresh flat-leaf
    parsley, chopped

potato wedges and green salad,
    to serve

Heat the oil in a heavy-based pan and fry the onions and peppers over a medium heat until they start to colour a little at the edges. This caramelisation will really enhance the smoky flavour of the dish so it is well worth taking your time over.

Add the garlic and smoked paprika and fry for 1 minute, then add the tomatoes and pour in the wine. Bring up to the boil and simmer, uncovered for 15–20 minutes until the sauce has reduced and thickened.

Whilst the stew is simmering make the almond and garlic sauce. Add the almonds to a dry frying pan and toast them for a couple of minutes, taking care not to burn them. As soon as they are golden, tip them into a food processor. Add the olive oil to the pan and fry the bread on both sides until crisp and golden. Remove to a plate and allow to cool for a few seconds, then crumble into the food processor. Add the garlic and parsley to the food processor and whizz everything together, adding just enough cold water to give you a smooth paste. Season with a little salt and black pepper and set aside.

Add the prawns to the thickened tomato sauce and simmer for a further 5 minutes or so until the prawns are cooked through. Remove from the heat and stir through the almond and garlic sauce. Taste to check the seasoning and add a little more salt and black pepper if necessary. Serve immediately with potato wedges and a green salad.

Not suitable for freezing.

Italian seafood stew with fried polenta wedges

This fresh fish stew is packed full of those classic ingredients – fresh basil, plum tomatoes, wine and garlic – that make Italian cuisine so loved by all. The great thing about it is you can use whatever fish and shellfish are available, there are no hard and fast rules. And that to me sums up the best of Italian cooking; you take what looks good on the day and you do very little to it to make it sing loud and clear.

Serves 4–6 | Takes 20 minutes to make, 40–45 minutes to cook

For the fried polenta wedges
150g quick-cook polenta
1 tbsp finely chopped fresh rosemary leaves
50g Parmesan cheese, grated
2–3 tbsp extra virgin olive oil
salt and freshly ground black pepper

For the stew
150ml red wine vinegar
2 large onions, finely chopped
3 tbsp olive oil
3 cloves garlic
200ml good-quality fish stock
200ml white wine
2 x 400g cans chopped plum tomatoes
2 wide strips of lemon peel
2 tsp dried oregano
650g white fish fillets eg cod, haddock or sea bass, cut into 5–6cm pieces
450g shellfish eg clams, mussels, shell-on raw prawns, thoroughly washed
large bunch of fresh basil, leaves roughly torn

Begin by preparing the polenta as it needs time to set. Bring 600ml water to a steady boil in a large pan and pour in the polenta, stirring continuously. Add the rosemary, Parmesan, olive oil and a good seasoning of salt and black pepper. Cook carefully for around 3–4 minutes, it will bubble and splutter. Pour into a well-oiled shallow tin and set aside to cool and set.

Place the vinegar and onion in a large, heavy-based pan, with a lid, and boil them together for around 5 minutes, or until the vinegar has virtually evaporated. Add the oil and garlic and fry for a few minutes.

Pour in the stock, wine and the tomatoes and bring to a gentle simmer. Add the lemon peel and oregano and season well with salt and pepper. Simmer, uncovered for around 20 minutes or until the onions are soft and the sauce has reduced.

Lay the fish fillets on the surface of the stew and cover with the lid. Cook for 5 minutes before adding the shellfish. Re-cover and cook for a further 5 minutes or so by which time the fish should be opaque and cooked through and the shellfish should have opened. Remove from the heat and gently stir through the torn basil. Cover and set aside while you fry the polenta.

Heat a griddle pan to searing hot. Cut the polenta into triangles and brush each side generously with olive oil. Griddle the triangles for a couple of minutes or so on either side until crisp and golden.

Taste the stew to check the seasoning and serve immediately with the polenta wedges on the side.

Not suitable for freezing.

Saffron pork with wild garlic

Wild garlic can be hard to find but for those precious few weeks in spring when it can be bought or foraged I think it is well worth making the effort to use it. The subtle garlic taste and a spinach-like texture make it an endlessly useful ingredient. In this earthy spring stew it is combined with pork and saffron to create a delicious seasonal dish that is great with chewy brown rice. Out of season, you could add an extra clove of garlic and substitute spinach instead.

Serves 4–6 | Takes 20 minutes to make, about 40 minutes to cook

1 heaped tbsp plain flour
900g pork tenderloin, cut into 2cm slices
2 tbsp olive oil
2 onions, finely sliced
1 clove garlic, crushed
175ml white wine
500ml chicken stock
pinch of saffron threads
2 generous handfuls of wild garlic leaves, thoroughly washed
salt and freshly ground black pepper
brown rice, to serve

Season the flour with salt and freshly ground black pepper. On a large plate, sprinkle the seasoned flour over the pork and toss well to coat evenly.

Heat the oil in a heavy-based pan, with a lid, and quickly brown the meat on both sides. Transfer the meat to a plate and set aside.

Lower the heat a little and fry the onions until they are soft and translucent. Add the garlic and fry for a further minute before pouring in the wine. Reduce the wine at a steady simmer, scraping the base of the pan to release the flavoursome sticky bits of pork and onion.

Return the meat to the pan, pour over the stock and sprinkle in the saffron threads. Bring up to a gentle simmer, cover and cook for 1 hour. Remove the lid, stir through the garlic leaves and season with salt and black pepper. Cook, uncovered, for 10–15 minutes until the garlic leaves have wilted and the sauce is thickened.

Taste to check the seasoning, adjust if necessary and serve spooned over brown rice.

Freeze for up to 3 months. Defrost overnight in the fridge before reheating thoroughly, adding a little water if it seems a little dry.

Spanish chicken with peppers and olives

Smoked paprika is a quintessentially Spanish ingredient that I adore, but it is best used sparingly as the taste can become overpowering if used too liberally. I like to eat this with saffron-infused rice.

Serves 4–6 |Takes 20 minutes to make, 1½ hours to cook

2 tbsp plain flour
900g chicken thighs, bone in
2 tbsp olive oil
2 onions, sliced
1 red pepper, deseeded and sliced
1 green pepper, deseeded and
  sliced
3 cloves garlic, crushed
1 tsp smoked paprika
200ml red wine
400ml chicken stock
6 tomatoes, chopped
generous handful of black olives
bunch of fresh flat-leaf parsley,
  roughly chopped
salt and freshly ground black
  pepper
saffron rice, to serve

Season the flour with salt and freshly ground black pepper. On a large plate, toss the chicken pieces in the seasoned flour to get a good, even coating.

Heat the oil in a large, heavy-based pan, with a lid, and fry the chicken pieces in two or three batches until they are crisp and golden on both sides. Return all the browned chicken to the pan, along with the onions and peppers. Continue to fry for a few minutes until the vegetables begin to soften then add the garlic and smoked paprika and stir well.

Pour in the wine and chicken stock, along with the tomatoes and bring slowly up to a steady simmer. Cover with a lid and cook gently for around 1½ hours by which time the chicken should be coming away from the bone and the sauce should be thickened. Check after 1 hour or so and if the sauce is still quite thin remove the lid for the final 30 minutes of cooking.

Stir through the olives and parsley and taste to check the seasoning. Remove from the heat and serve immediately with the saffron rice.

Not suitable for freezing.

FISH

Lemon sole with ginger and lemongrass

This is a super light and healthy stew. Delicate fillets of lemon sole are gently poached on top of a broth fragrant with lemongrass, ginger and garlic. You could use fillets of plaice, or even halibut if you wanted to push the boat out and treat yourself.

Serves 4–6 | Takes 20 minutes to make, about 40 minutes to cook

1 tbsp vegetable oil
160g shallots, finely sliced
2 lemongrass stalks, quartered
  lengthways
3 cloves garlic, crushed
60g fresh root ginger, peeled and
  finely grated
1.2 litres fish stock
1–2 tbsp laksa paste or Thai curry
  paste
1 tbsp nam pla (fish sauce)
1 tbsp soy sauce
350g dried egg noodles (allow
  1 block per person)
200g pak choi, sliced through the
  root
4–6 lemon sole fillets, halved if
  they are large
salt and freshly ground black
  pepper
lime juice, to taste
small bunch of fresh coriander,
  chopped, to garnish

Heat the oil in a large, wide heavy-based pan and gently fry the shallots until they are soft and starting to colour at the edges. Add the lemongrass, garlic and ginger and fry for 1 minute.

Pour over the stock and add the laksa paste, nam pla and soy sauce. Bring up to the boil and simmer, uncovered, for 15 minutes.

Add the noodles, breaking up and separating them as they begin to soften. Then add the pak choi and simmer for 2 minutes. Give the stew a good stir to make sure the noodles have separated, then carefully lay the fillets on top of the stew, spooning a little of the liquid over them. Cover with the lid and simmer for 5 minutes or until the fish is cooked through.

Taste to check the seasoning you may want to add a little salt and black pepper – and add enough lime juice to sharpen it to your liking. Serve in deep bowls sprinkled with the chopped coriander.

Not suitable for freezing.

Chicken cacciatore

This Italian classic is best made at the end of the summer when there is a glut of really ripe tomatoes. It is great served with rosemary roast new potatoes and a simple rocket salad.

Serves 4–6 | Takes 15 minutes to make, 1$\frac{1}{2}$ hours to cook

1 large chicken, approx. 2kg, jointed into 6 pieces
2 tbsp olive oil
2 onions, thickly sliced
3 cloves garlic, crushed
2 tbsp chopped fresh sage leaves
700g ripe tomatoes
boiling water, to skin tomatoes
200ml chicken stock
175ml white wine
salt and freshly ground black pepper

For the crispy sage leaves
25g unsalted butter
1 tbsp extra virgin olive
12 fresh age leaves, torn in half

rosemary roast new potatoes and rocket salad, to serve

Heat the oil in a large, heavy-based pan, with a lid, and fry the chicken in very hot oil in two batches until it is golden on both sides. Remove to a plate and set aside.

Lower the heat and add the onions, garlic and chopped sage and fry for a few minutes until soft.

Whilst the onions are softening, skin the tomatoes by scoring round their middle with a sharp knife and submerging them in boiling water for 2 minutes. Drain, slip the skins off and chop coarsely. You can remove the seeds as well if you wish I generally leave them in as I find they add plenty of flavour.

Return the chicken to the pan along with the chopped tomatoes, stock and wine. Bring up to a gentle simmer, cover and cook for about 1 hour. Remove the lid from the pan and cook for a further 30 minutes to allow the sauce to gently reduce.

Whilst the chicken is cooking make the crispy sage leaves by melting the butter with the oil in a small frying pan. When the butter begins to foam add the sage leaves and fry for a few minutes until crisp. Drain on kitchen paper.

When the stew has finished cooking taste to check the seasoning and adjust if necessary. Garnish with the crispy sage leaves and serve with the rosemary roast new potatoes and rocket salad.

Freeze for up to 3 months. Defrost overnight in the fridge before reheating thoroughly, adding a little water if it seems a little dry.

Braised courgettes and tomatoes

I think of this as an 'end of the summer' stew, showcasing all the things that taste great at that time of year. For me it's the perfect thing for a light lunch, preferably in the garden, served with hunks of crusty bread to mop up the sweet juices.

Serves 4–6 | Takes 10 minutes to make, about 15 minutes to cook

2 tbsp olive oil
6 courgettes (small ones are best), cut into finger-sized batons
3 cloves garlic, sliced
175ml white wine
6 large tomatoes, roughly chopped
1 tbsp sun-dried tomato purée
lemon juice, to taste
generous handful of mixed chopped fresh herbs eg mint, parsley, basil, chives and marjoram
salt and freshly ground pepper
extra virgin olive oil, to drizzle
crusty bread, to serve

Heat the oil gently in a large, wide pan and fry the courgettes and garlic for 5 minutes until they start to soften but not colour. Pour in the wine and let it bubble to reduce a little, then add the tomatoes and sun-dried tomato purée. Season generously with salt and black pepper and simmer, uncovered for about 10–15 minutes by which time the courgettes should be tender and the tomatoes reduced to a delicious thick sauce.

Remove from the heat and let cool a little this is one of those dishes that tastes better when heading towards room temperature rather than piping hot. Stir though the lemon juice to taste and the fresh herbs, taste to check the seasoning and drizzle with plenty of your best extra virgin olive oil. Serve with crusty bread.

Not suitable for freezing.

Calamari and white wine stew

This stew somehow manages to be light and rich at the same time, and has the added bonus that it still tastes great when eaten the day after it was made, which makes it perfect for a lazy summer lunch in the garden with friends. I like to serve it tossed through a mountain of spaghetti.

Serves 4–6 | Takes 10 minutes to make, 25–40 minutes to cook

4 tbsp olive oil
2 onions, very finely chopped
4 cloves garlic, crushed
pinch dried chilli flakes
350g cherry tomatoes, halved
300ml dry white wine
1kg squid, cut into bite-size pieces and scored
generous handful of fresh flat-leaf parsley, chopped
juice of 1 lemon
salt and freshly ground black pepper
spaghetti, to serve

Heat the olive oil in a large, wide pan, a deep frying pan is ideal, and gently sweat the onions for around 5 minutes or until they are soft and translucent but not at all brown. Stir through the garlic and chilli and cook for 1 minute.

Add the tomatoes and the wine and a generous seasoning of salt and freshly ground black pepper. Bring up to a steady simmer and cook, uncovered, for 20 minutes or so until the sauce has thickened and the tomatoes are pulpy.

Turn the heat down to the minimum and add the prepared squid. Cook, uncovered, until the squid is tender when pricked with a fork. The time this takes will really vary depending on the size of the squid you used it could be 5 minutes, or it could be 20, so keep on checking.

Remove from the heat and stir through the parsley and lemon juice. Taste to check the seasoning and adjust if necessary. Serve with spaghetti.

Not suitable for freezing.

British and American cookbooks use different measuring systems. In the UK, dry ingredients are measured by weight, with the metric system increasingly replacing the Imperial one, while in the US they are measured by volume.

Weight

7g	¼ ounce	200g	7 ounces
20g	¾ ounce	220–225g	8 ounces
25–30g	1 ounce	250–260g	9 ounces
40g	1½ ounces	300g	10½ ounces
50g	1¾ ounces	325g	11½ ounces
60–65g	2¼ ounces	350g	12 ounces
70–75g	2½ ounces	400g	14 ounces
80g	2¾ ounces	450g	1 pound
90g	3¼ ounces	500g	1 pound 2 ounces
100g	3½ ounces	600g	1 pound 5 ounces
110–115g	4 ounces	700g	1 pound 9 ounces
120–130g	4½ ounces	750g	1 pound 10 ounces
140g	5 ounces	800g	1¾ pounds
150g	5½ ounces	900g	2 pounds
175–180g	6 ounces	1kg	2¼ pounds

Volume

50ml	1¾ fl oz	300ml	10 fl oz
60ml	2 fl oz (4 tablespoons/¼ cup)	350ml	12 fl oz
75ml	2½ fl oz (5 tablespoons)	400ml	14 fl oz
90ml	3 fl oz (⅜ cup)	450ml	15 fl oz
100ml	3½ fl oz	475ml	16 fl oz (2 cups)
125ml	4 fl oz (½ cup)	500ml	18 fl oz
150ml	5 fl oz (⅔ cup)	600ml	20 fl oz
175ml	6 fl oz	800ml	28 fl oz
200ml	7 fl oz	850ml	30 fl oz
250ml	8 fl oz (1 cup)	1 litre	35 fl oz (4 cups)

Length

5mm	¼ inch	8cm	3¼ inches
1cm	½ inch	9cm	3½ inches
2cm	¾ inch	10cm	4 inches
2.5cm	1 inch	12cm	4½ inches
3cm	1¼ inches	14cm	5½ inches
4cm	1½ inches	20cm	8 inches
5cm	2 inches	24cm	9½ inches
6cm	2½ inches	30cm	12 inches